The East Riding of Yorkshire with Hull and York

A Portrait

by

A. G. Dickens

Edited and with an introduction by

John Markham

Highgate of Beverley

Highgate Publications (Beverley) Limited
2002

British Library Cataloguing in Publication Data.
A catalogue record for this book is available from the British
Library.

© 2002 The executors of the estate of the late A. G. Dickens

The executors of the estate of the late A. G. Dickens assert
his moral right to be identified as the author of this work.

ISBN 1 902645 33 2

Published by

Highgate of Beverley

Highgate Publications (Beverley) Limited
4 Newbegin, Beverley, HU17 8EG. Telephone (01482) 886017

Printed by Highgate Print Limited
4 Newbegin, Beverley, HU17 8EG. Telephone (01482) 886017

Contents

Cover pictures:

(front) Bishop Wilton (JDL)

(back) Souttergate, Hedon (JDL)

Abbreviations used in captions:

JG.-John Goode

JDL.-John D. Lucock

List of Colour Illustrations

1. Howden Minster: the chapter house
2. Beneath the Ouse Bridge, M62.
3. York Castle.
4. The Shambles, York.
5. York, Bootham Bar.
6. South Cave.
7. East Yorkshire harvest: near Bishop Wilton.
8. Wilberfoss.
9. An East Yorkshire seascape: Flamborough.
10. Old Town, Bridlington.
11. Rudston Monolith in All Saints churchyard.
12. Hull Fair.

13. Trinity House, Hull.
14. Hull's Garden Village.
15. The Marina, Hull.
16. Riverhead, Driffield.
17. Skipsea Castle motte.
18. Sunk Island, looking towards Ottringham church: the great skies of Holderness.
19. Beverley Beck.
20. North Bar Without, Beverley.
21. St. Mary's Church, Beverley: Victorian flying buttresses on the medieval south transept.
22. Beverley's Georgian Market Cross, Saturday Market.
23. Newbegin, Beverley: one of Beverley's fine Georgian streets.
24. New Walk, Beverley.

Introduction

to the Second Edition

by

John Markham

Arthur Geoffrey Dickens (1910-2001), the son of a Hull dockland foreman, made his way by scholarship from Wheeler Street council school to the City's only public school, Hymers College, where his outstanding ability was recognised by its renowned history master, 'Alfie' Birtles, who steered him successfully through an Oxford scholarship. After displaying brilliance in his undergraduate years, he was elected Fellow and Tutor of Keble College in 1933, the first phase of a distinguished academic career in which he gained international recognition as the leading authority on the English Reformation, and which was to be crowned by his appointment to the Chair of Modern History at King's College, London University, in 1962 and the Directorship of the Institute of Historical Research in 1967.

But earlier, from 1949-62, he was back on home territory as Professor of History at what was, first, Hull University College and, from 1954, Hull University. He could now revisit his roots, walk more often on the Wolds and look again at the familiar scenes of childhood with a perception intensified by his absence both in Oxford and the army and with the added dimension of mature scholarship which enabled him to see the East Riding within the context of national and European history.

Hull already had a long tradition of local history with well-supported adult education classes conducted by such popular lecturers as W. Foot Walker, F. W. Brooks and K. A. MacMahon, and in the post-war years the stream of local publications was emerging at a pace which quickened into a torrent in the later 20th century. In contributing another volume Dickens had no intention of producing a humourless, fact-loaded, chronological history. As he made clear in his manifesto-like foreword, his book was to be 'a character sketch of the East Riding . . . admittedly personal, impressionist and selective'. His aim was to stimulate rather than instruct, to persuade his readers to look more intensely at familiar places and to reflect more deeply on what they had seen.

As a book written with the unashamed subjectivity which historians are expected to shun and as a loving, though not uncritical, tribute from a loyal son, it differs from the later more weighty tomes on which his reputation rests. Dickens surveyed East Yorkshire from prehistoric times to the post-war period, always aware of the relationship between landscape and people and of the hints of a distant past still surfacing in the language and the character of its inhabitants. History, to most of his readers, was a book-based subject, but Dickens showed the importance of intelligent observation and sensitive interpretation: scenery and buildings were clues to the past as revealing as documents.

The years in academia had not dimmed the clarity of his perception. People and events were viewed with a freshness which contrasted with the conventional phraseology of historians who were less acute. The Tudor chronicler, John Leland, he dismissed, first, as 'leaden-spirited but supremely industrious', and, later, as 'our heavy uncle', and 'saturnine'; Beverley Minster's much vaunted right of sanctuary he condemned as 'sacred thuggery'; and his scorn for admirers of the popular Victorian composer, Stainer, was neatly conveyed by his approval of the efforts made by Yorkshire choirs 'gradually contriving' to abandon his works in favour of Bach and Handel. There was wickedly donnish humour in his expressed preference for the 'sinuous realism' of the 'lower limbs' of the females depicted on the Hotham tomb in South Dalton church over the 'standardised and tiresome anatomical ideal' conveyed in 'a million stocking-advertisements'. His opinions, not least his lack of enthusiasm for the architecture of York

Minister, were not clouded by diplomatic verbiage, though he self-deprecatingly admitted a tendency to digress and moralise.

Dickens had a talent for the telling phrase which vividly captured the atmosphere of a place or scene. Houghton Hall and its park he saw as 'the perfect background for a group by Arthur Devis', while Cottingham was the nearest the East Riding would ever come to having a Latin Quarter. He was very sensitive to the distinctive atmosphere of Holderness. Evocative names like Ulrome, Nunkeeling, Boreas Hill and Spurn were, he felt, 'charged with music and poetry', and filled with the spirit of 'crumbling shores and drowned churches, of a vast tidal estuary with endless weedy mud flats, of cities thrown up, then swallowed by the waves'. His style, at times a little too literary for modern tastes, could rival that of J. B. Priestley when he touched on a topic where a patriotic heart overwhelmed the feeble objections of reason: 'only a bigoted observer will fail to recognise the truth that authentic Yorkshire pudding seldom emerges out of the county of its origin'.

In spite of his criticism of the Hull he saw on his return in 1949, his love for its Old Town glows on his pages. He knew more about its history than he did as boy but he had not forgotten lingering in Ye Olde White Harte ('despising my puerile glass of lemonade') while his father chatted in the forbidden smoke room with merchants and sea captains. Not far away was Hepworth's Arcade with two of the delights of his youth, the Penny Bazaar, and, 'at the tunnel's lowest point', the Ecclesiastical Repository. One of his grandfathers had watched Alexandra Dock being built and later become its chief inspector, while the other was a Primitive Methodist local preacher, 'resplendent in silk hat, morning coat, gold Albert and side whiskers', who lovingly took his little grandson's hand on their way to chapel.

East Yorkshire in the 1950s was, as he says, still very rural, and, even if his comments challenged received opinion, the picture he drew was of a traditional society, with its focus primarily on the countryside, the churches and the great houses which remained private homes. He did not attach the importance to Georgian architecture accorded by the innumerable books and articles which have appeared since he wrote. Hull's High Street, 18th-century Beverley and Hedon would now deservedly receive far more attention. Victorian architecture, then generally undervalued, was another subject which now attracts praise; 19th-century public buildings, housing developments such as Hull's Avenues, as well as parks and railways, feature prominently in more recent publications. He was, however, more alert than many to the advantages of original modern architecture over 'the dull, anonymous brick box'.

Post-war England was drab, ruin from the war lay all around, memories of near annihilation were vivid and the future indistinct. Many talked, somewhat unconfidently, of the day when things would get back to normal, a blissful state never to be achieved. Dickens was pessimistic about the decline in cultural standards which he witnessed, though these were to be regarded with retrospective envy when even greater social changes occurred. He had fears, too, for the future of the great houses, which he saw as embodiments of cultural and spiritual values. No one, in 1954, could have predicted the country house mania which had gathered an unstoppable momentum in the later part of the century, the growing influence of English Heritage and the National Trust, and what has become a history industry in which television has played a conspicuous part. Many buildings and places, like Burton Constable Hall and High Street, Hull, are in far better condition today than they were 50 years ago: so much so that the over-used word, heritage, can raise a cynical response.

The passing of time has given added value to the book. As well as fulfilling the author's aim of creating a portrait of the area from the perspective of the early 1950s, it has become a bench-mark by which one can assess the impact of the succeeding half-century. Almost every page deserves a commentary on things which have changed, sometimes for the worse but not infrequently for the better. In the event, footnotes have been restricted to points considered to be of particular relevance or interest. A few minor typographical errors in the original edition have been corrected; some of the lengthier digressions have been abbreviated; and Suggestions for Further Reading, outdated by the proliferation of local historical publications since 1954, omitted. Some of these works are referred to in the footnotes. The new photographs in this edition illustrate some places mentioned by Dickens and others which an author writing today might choose to include.

Foreword

This character-sketch of the East Riding is admittedly personal, impressionist and selective; it seeks to stimulate rather than to instruct. It is intended for non-specialist readers, but less for race-goers than for thoughtful wanderers. It strives to avoid certain assumptions still rather prevalent in such books, namely that the reader is incapable of thinking in high gear, hates ideas while adoring facts for their own sake, has lost every vestige of natural humour and somehow in youth suffered complete spiritual atrophy. Having discussed these topics with hundreds of general readers, both in Britain and in the United States, I find singularly few of them measuring up to these grim specifications. Hence I conclude that writers who seek to arouse interest in topography and local history should be no more ponderous than Nature made them, should remember that people are more often bored by cold mutton than by Sidney Smith's favourite dish, *pâté de fois gras*, eaten to the sound of trumpets.

I am indebted to my friends Mr K. A. MacMahon and Mr J. M. Meadley for reading the proofs and making some valuable corrections. Of late years I have benefited from the table talk of my colleague Mr F. W. Brooks, who in matters of the East Riding is the undoubted 'master of those who know'. Needless to say, none of these gentlemen bears responsibility for any errors which may remain.

The University,
Hull.
December, 1954.

Prologue

The East Riding countryside betrays not a few feminine characteristics: it is gentle, adaptable, highly receptive, inviting the approach of man and outwardly amenable to his rough caress, yet withal persuasive and pertinacious, steeling an innermost heart against radical change and possession. So far from dominating or crushing its people, this land has imposed only that mild sway which is half an invitation to conquest and achievement. Nevertheless, all its invaders – crude Anglian warrior, heathen Danish marauder, mail-hearted Norman land-hunter – all have been transformed inside a generation or two by the spell of marsh, wold and estuary, the voices which, perhaps even more insistently than those of prophets and lawgivers, have prevailed against our turbulent ancestry and made us the mild-mannered farmers and shepherds and traders of these later centuries.

The composite picture evoked by these words East Riding remains intensely rural: the square-cut farm of old brick and tile, the line of cottages – one of them unconvincingly disguised as store and post-office – sloping down the grass-fringed street to the murky village pond; the chickens scratching in the sun, the old woman pegging out the washing, which flies with wild half-human gestures above the rank hollyhocks, the girl calling in the child to tea and, beyond them all, the telegraph poles climbing toward the chalk wold, whereon a dark plantation breasts the crystal wind from the sea. Yet equally the mind's symbolic backcloth might show a forlorn house, full of the roar of the waves, the last survivor of a dead township upon a wasting coast of clay. Again, it might reveal a fat potato-laden fen traversed by a sluggish river, or the grandest wall of cliffs in England, or again the coronets or her fairest minster glimpsed across a stray glade from the vanished forests of Deira. And to many a native, as to myself when young, the Riding will most readily suggest a skyline of blue woods and a windmill beckoning toward a high window across the slates of the city whose demeaning embrace he may all too seldom elude. In truth, the tilt and twist of the land, a process lasting here into modern times, has created a province unusually complex for its extent, and one which even that superficial and prosaic informant, the relief map, quite correctly divides into three major regions: the levels of the Vale of York; the Wolds and the coastal plain of Holderness.

This Riding is shaped like a half-opened fan, its delicate handle at Spurn, one straight edge formed by the Humber, the other by the North Sea. Derwent and Ouse demarcate the rounded outer edge of the fan, for the former of these boundary rivers actually takes its rise in patient streams springing but a few yards behind the sea-cliff at Filey, yet needing a roundabout hundred-mile journey to attain the sea. Across the centre of this area swing the Wolds, the last stretch of that longest of the four chalk tentacles radiating from Salisbury Plain, the tentacle which is jointed by Thames, Wash and Humber, then finally broken off by the ocean itself at Flamborough Head. But a more absorbing and poetic picture of the land is drawn by the geologist, who sees the rocks of Yorkshire ranging from the ancient silurians of the western Pennines to the recent glacial deposits of Holderness, sees them laid, aeon after aeon, in downward slope from west to east, and overlapping like a pack of cards swept over from left to right by the sudden gesture of a conjuror, when he invites you to select one from the table.

The broad stretch of triassic red sandstone which forms the floor of the Vale of York is now covered by fertile alluvial deposits and by the prisoners – boulder clay, drift and moraines – which a great glacier had to release when at last, like a routed army, it retreated to the north. Hence the curious island-hill now crowned by the church of Holme-upon-Spalding-Moor is in fact an unusually hard triassic mound which has defied glacier and flood to form the chief landmark of the lower Vale. Farther eastward, beyond a narrower strip of lias, the chalk slab of the Wolds lies several hundred feet thick and covered by a shallow surface soil, habituated only in recent times to the plough.

Before the Ice Age, when a mighty sub-tropical fauna ruled the land, the sea used to wash a line of cliffs along the present eastern edge of the Wolds, from Sewerby in the north through Driffield and Bishop Burton to Hessle in the south, cliffs now far inland and subterranean, their sharp plunge to sea-level masked by the soft contours of later accretions. As for the glacial sands, clays and gravels of Holderness – the extreme right-hand card of our pack – they were deposited, geologically speaking, but yesterday and are rich in the relics of yesterday's children; the mammoth and the primeval ox, the walrus, seal and reindeer, together with a numerous mollusca of arctic type, doubtless dragged from the bed of the North Sea as the ice advanced from Scandinavia to build this coastal plain.

Thus was the stage set for the appearance of neolithic man, herald of an enterprise, thereafter continuous, of a tenacious humanity, whose monuments, standing in thick profusion upon every square mile of the Riding, will command our chief attentions throughout the rest of this book. At first man made ditches and mounds along the hills; presently he came down and began clearing the forest for tillage. He laboured upon military roads, camps and villas for his Mediterranean overlords. He either served, or fled from, those three waves of invaders who so adroitly merged with the landscape, though doubtless they came already predisposed to abandon the storm-wanderer Wotan for the scholastic Augustine, the Dyonisian for the Apollonian, the midsummer sacrifice of the war-band for the rationalised mysteries of the Mass. These new men, blending into a harmonious stock, speedily resumed the bonds of church, manor and court of justice, traded in timber, wool and corn, painfully relearned much Latin wisdom and achieved the delicate equilibria, both spiritual and physical, of gothic architecture. Finally, the years since about 1700 have

seen us decisively speeding the attack on our environment: we have drained the long marshlands of Humber, Hull and Derwent, turned even the high sheep-walks into neat, prosperous farms, hunted the whale across the Arctic, realised, with more debatable wisdom, a new Iron Age in a network of railways and in the third port of the Kingdom. Nowhere more pretentiously than across the pages of the East Riding has man written his proud title, ' minister and interpreter of nature'.

Yet always has he been torn between the rival voices of earth and sea, for the East Riding has long been a maritime province, sharing the trade and fisheries of two great salt lakes along with men of several other nations. Most of these stand quite closely related by blood and speech; all have needed but the common pursuit of the sea to unite them in a kinship which has survived many a state-war and liberated many a man from that isolationism so fashionable, so fatal, since the time Shakespeare prated about 'this blessed plot'. And we who were bred in these seaboard places can still sometimes take pride in our allegiance to a 'natural' international culture, feel the old affinities with a mysterious power not shared by every Englishman, feel deeply and profoundly at home in the society of Bergen or Copenhagen, in the Hanseatic cities of Lower Saxony and even in far Helsingfors, at home as we never may in Wessex or Wales or Kensington.

So the quintessential attraction of the East Riding lies neither in its people nor in its scenery, but rather in a vividly expressed mingling of the two, in creative response to the challenges of the land and of the sea which washes its shores.

What faculties then, should a man possess to enjoy this waiting and unspoiled inheritance? He must first acquire some sense of time and the grandeur of our provincial story. He should know a little about gothic architecture and warm somewhat to the contour of ancient barrow and earthwork upon the wold. He should have an ear for dialect, a relish for that curious blend of hard-headedness and whimsy in the mind of a people steeped for centuries in the various Christian cults, yet to this day not altogether emancipated from folklore and superstition. He should have developed a taste for the not-quite-obvious in the natural scene, for the dappled and capricious day in spring, for the cold sea-wind of the North on the bare brow of the ridge, for the gentle melancholy of infinite mudflats and mirrors down an estuary broad to the horizon, for the slow drama of a receding shore which has left a score of churches engulfed in the sea. Above all, he must come to the East Riding freed from the grosser guidebook clichés and comparisons, must look at it as a thing quite individual, look at it innocent of any exclusive Cotswold or Kentish or Lake District standards of beauty, for the shires of England are a very diverse family of magicians, wherein the stillest minds run deepest and the quiet brother knows best the word which will unlock the hearts of men.

The vale and the city

Concerning the broad plain between the Wolds and the Ouse it would seem impertinent to write with the slightest suspicion of rhapsody. Rather must the mind, if it would rest in tune with its environment, dwell on the image of a potato, or, if it is an incurably dynamic mind, upon hedging, ditching, manuring, marling and all such indisputably good, laborious and useful works of man. Both physically and metaphorically, this is a flat land wherein the traveller soon calls for wheels – I had almost written wings – to flit speedily between those few places deserving prolonged attention. Only thrice does the dead level break – at Holme-upon-Spalding-Moor, the island hill just off the Wolds, and in the two crescentic moraines running through Escrick and York, both debris of the great glacier which once filled the Vale.

The several fens were drained at no very distant date and those near Selby remain subject to disastrous floods. Holme itself once formed a miniature Isle of Ely, while Walling Fen further south was thus described by Leland, the leaden-spirited but supremely industrious topographer of Henry VIII: 'From Northcave to Scalby a 3 miles, all by low Marsch and Medow Ground . . . This Fenne is communely caullid Waullyng Fenne and hath many Carres of Waters in it: and is so bigge that 58 Villages ly in and butting of it . . . The Fenne is 16 Miles in Cumpace.' Though these southern districts of the Vale of York can hardly boast the strong-souled, melancholy attraction of the Lincolnshire Fens, they share not a little of their general aspect and agrarian characteristics: the neat, businesslike farms with their square-cut buildings; the lack of woodlands, the network of deep ditches, and – most markedly in the warped lands by Ouse and Humber – the same phenomenal productivity. Inland, the lighter and sandier soils grow fine King Edwards and Majestics, with oats or rye, rather than wheat, as a secondary crop. But the extreme mobility of the lightest soils can cause havoc if gales accompany the seedling stage, the innocent townsman finding himself expected to believe stories of carrot-seed being sown in one parish but coming up in the next!

Though in recent years certain factories, seed-crushing, sugar-beet and so forth, have sprung up in the area immediately adjoining Selby on our Ouse frontier, the Vale remains overwhelmingly agricultural. Of its dwellers I hold a consistent if doubtless over-simplified impression: that of worthy, plodding farm-workers, square and angular as their houses and fields, less mentally isolated, but also less verbally picturesque and rich in local flavour than their compatriots of Holderness and the Wolds.

Yet how rash I was to ring down the curtain upon enthusiasm, for I must raise it the moment I come to speak of Howden, which dull little town happens to enclose a work glorious even in a gothic Elysium. This building belongs indeed not to the category of mere parish churches, but to that of collegiate minsters. The thirteenth and fourteenth centuries saw its erection in the grand manner of such foundations, the process much assisted by the highly providential emergence of a local saint, whose shrine attracted rich gifts from all quarters. No sooner had the choir been completed to house the remains of this useful Canon John, when the ambitious prebendaries demolished it and built one even loftier and more ornate. Yet this structure, half the length of the original church, fell to neglect when the Reformation had demoted the church to mere parochial status; its vaulting finally collapsed in 1696 and left everything east of the great central tower a majestic rain-mellowed ruin. On its south side, in almost equal decay, stands the octagonal chapter house, built by Chaucer's contemporary Bishop Skirlaw of Durham in a style halfway between the old Decorated and the new Perpendicular, a little masterpiece exquisite beyond all verbal analysis. The canons of Howden continued active until about 1500, when they completed the uppermost section of this central tower, which dominates flat Howdenshire almost as Boston Stump dominates the eastern Fens. The intact nave and transepts now form a large Early Decorated parish church, housing a wealth of arcading, sculptures, inscriptions and tombs. Among the last will be observed that of Sir Peter de Saltmarshe, who died in 1338 and whose direct descendants have held continuous sway at nearby Saltmarshe into this mid-twentieth century.[1] Two aspects of Howden church enjoy deserved fame: that from the market place with the ruined choir in its frame of old brick houses, and that from the far south-west corner of the churchyard. From this latter angle one may best study the four small hexagonal turrets which endow this quite unusual exterior with its peculiar grace. Only after some minutes does one mark the consummate skill of the unknown artist, who, placing the inner pair of turrets at a different angle from the outer, gains a complex pattern of light and shade, a variety in unity. This particular stroke may not, for all I know, be quite original at Howden, but the general evidence proves that these Yorkshire builders of the age of Edward III, so far from borrowing French tricks, stood rather in a position to reverse the debt.

A man who visits Howdenshire for pleasure will normally have little in mind beyond the architecture of Howden, Hemingbrough and Selby, yet possessing such interests he will do well to remember the Percy stronghold at Wressle, even though it was partially destroyed by the Roundheads and subsequently in 1796 gutted by fire. The *Gentleman's Magazine* of this latter date attributes the accident to 'the wilful carelessness of a Goth who resided in it and who appears not to have any notion of preserving what the democratic miscreants of Cromwell had the grace to spare'. Readers familiar with the bewigged idiom of that splendid age will need no reminder that the 'Goth' was a mere East Riding farmer and 'democratic' a distinct term of abuse.

Wressle was originally one of those quadrangular fortified manor houses which spread across the face of the North like a rash – the symptom of fatal disease in medieval society. Only the south side has survived, together with the shells of two massive square towers. 'One thing I liked exceedingly yn one of the Towers,' writes our heavy uncle Leland, 'that was a study caullid *Paradise*, wher was a closet in the midle of 8 Squares latisid aboute: and at the Toppe of every Square was a Desk ledgid to set Bookes on Cofers withyn them, and these seemid as joined hard to the Toppe of the Closet; and yet by Pulling, one or al wold cum downe, briste highe in rabettes (grooves), and serve for Deskes to lay Bokes on.' Very shortly before Leland's visit, Wressle had been one of the two great houses of the Percies, Earls of Northumberland. Its arrangements, elaborate as those of a royal court, are set out in the famous Northumberland Household Book, originally compiled for the 'Magnificent' Fifth Earl about 1512. With this in mind I first approached these bare walls one quiet-coloured autumn evening and tried to think back through four hundred years, to visualise the old pageantry – the fifty daily guests, the two hundred menials under the galaxy of great household officers, the minstrels, the chaplains, the wagon-loads of tapestry and furniture, the vast kitchens and stables, the gargantuan consumption of game and venison, Where a multitude of men breathed joy and woe

> Long ago . . .
> Now, the single little turret that remains
> On the plains,
> By the caper overrooted, by the gourd
> Overscored,
> While the patching houseleek's head of
>   blossom winks
> Through the chinks,
> Marks the basement whence a tower in
>   ancient time
> Sprang sublime . . .

But if Wressle might still enshrine *Love among the Ruins*, the other great Percy house of its period has left not one stone upon another. Leconfield, north of Beverley, a still larger and more splendid mansion, is now a mere field-site surrounded by the old moat, a space of preternatural largeness for a house and one which harbours ghosts even at noon.

A couple of miles beyond Wressle lies Hemingbrough, boasting like Howden a one-time collegiate church, later in foundation, architecturally much smaller and less lovely, yet a monument of great interest. Its stone spire just doubles the height of the squat tower supporting it, hence giving the whole church an ill-balanced air, the aspect of a thickset dwarf wearing an absurdly high sugarloaf hat. Around the tower runs a moulding formed by a line of washing tuns or tubs and representing a pun on the name of Prior Washington, who built this tower five hundred years ago. Inside is much fine medieval woodwork and the chantry chapel of the Babthorpes, the old family long resident at Osgodby in this once enormous parish. Having increased their fortunes by buying monastic lands, these Babthorpes subsequently reverted to Romanism, defied the penal laws and concealed here the Jesuits whose secret ministrations bound many local families to that faith. Their women, as so often with the old Roman Catholic families of Yorkshire, proved more steadfast and audacious than their men and it was chiefly Lady Grace Babthorpe who ruined the family by incurring enormous fines and prison-sentences for herself and her relatives.[2] Before Queen Elizabeth died, the Babthorpes were selling their lands, much like the family of Guy Fawkes, himself a York man with Hemingbrough connections. So the Lady Grace, her husband, Sir Ralph, and her son, Sir William, all died exiled in the Low Countries, she as a widowed nun of Louvain and Sir William as a penniless soldier fighting in the service of Catholic Spain. Of these last and very novelish Babthorpes we naturally see little sign among the homely memorials at Hemingbrough. From thence into Selby I cannot follow my reader without committing a wanton territorial aggression against the West Riding[3] and I must merely remark that, if he has read only the conventional books, he will find its Abbey quite unexpectedly wonderful.

Northward from Selby we traverse a land of brick villages, smiling crops and long water-meadows to the very gates of York. Here is a Mesopotamia filled by the prosaic though diverse spirits of the two rivers: the Derwent meandering mildly between its oozy banks, the Ouse a broad, aggressive flood still attracting anglers, forlorn men perhaps deceived by William Harrison, one of those very river-conscious Elizabethans, who hardily avers that in his day the Ouse still produced 'a verie sweet fat and delicate samon'. Should their credulity extend thus far, they may well proceed to the passage where Harrison speaks of the narrow, unromantic River Hull as 'a streame abounding with sturgeon and lampreie'. And the oddest feature of all remains the fact that he was probably speaking the truth!

Of these comfortable, quiet Mesopotamian villages, Riccall last broke into history in 1066 as the scene of important Combined Operations. There it was that the gigantic King Harold Hardrada of Norway and Earl Tostig disembarked their troops from a navy of three hundred ships, marched on to capture York and thence out to Stamford Bridge, defeat and death, at the hands of Harold of England. Between Riccall and Skipwith extends a large flat common, perhaps the only part of the old heathlands between Ouse and Wold to retain its original characteristics, and upon it certain low mounds, islanded in pale green, break the dark heather and gorse. They constitute a typical lowland hut-circle of the mid-Bronze Age, for these ancient men, contrary to the general impression, settled somewhat commonly in such places, fearing not the plain as such, but the shades of the forest. Needless to

remark, the consistent Danomania of our popular archaeology has for centuries dubbed these tumuli 'Danes' Hills'. The tower of Skipwith church contains some of the best Saxon masonry in Yorkshire, the south door some fine medieval ironwork, though in this latter category it is certainly surpassed by its neighbour, the famous door of Stillingfleet. Even

A view of the Minster over the roofs of York.
(Donald Sheldon)

unbiased foreign experts place this last piece of oak and iron back in the eleventh century. Besides two great C-shaped hinges, two gesticulating human figures and some oddly international swastikas formed of fleurs-de-lys, this door clearly shows a long Viking ship with the steering paddle hanging over the stern! The Stillingfleet door has, of course, been connected by romantic writers with the roughly contemporary advent of Hardrada's fleet – an alleged piece of early illustrated journalism in which the heart simply yearns to believe. The doorway surrounding this venerable problem-child is a splendid Late Norman affair with five orders of beak-heads, zig-zags and animal designs in rich barbaric profusion, a doorway regarded as the classic exemplar of our so-called 'Yorkshire Norman' style.

From these river-lands we soon reach the shambling, unworthy, outer suburbs of York, a capital city which belongs to none of the three Ridings, yet concerning which I cannot out of sheer love and intimacy forbear to write a few paragraphs. And I recognise the venture as foolhardy, since York is no mere cathedral city, but a cross-section of the Western World, demanding, if due proportion be observed, an essay at least as long as the whole East Riding. There in the first century of our era the Romans founded a camp which soon became the greatest of their bases, dominating the restive northern tribes and holding back the painted barbarians behind the Wall. York was in turn the capital of the old Northumbrian Kingdom, the school from which Alcuin came to revise the higher education of the Carolingian Empire, the seat of medieval Kings and Parliaments, the centre of the Tudor Council in the North, tamer and breaker of those feudal complexes which offered the last internal threat to the sovereignty of our English state.

From this age, nevertheless, York's trade and manufactures fell into decline; it lay, perchance happily, outside the main orbits of the Industrial Revolution and during the last century recovered importance rather as the prime railway centre of the North. In its role of administrative, legal and ecclesiastical metropolis, York early developed a 'society' compounded of lawyers, doctors, churchmen and those northern gentry who maintained town houses or lodgings within its walls. Somewhat tragically, however, York failed in earlier times to establish a university, though for such it would have formed an excellent setting, wherein the young might hold converse with a glorious civilisation, almost unbroken since Roman times. It petitioned to become the seat of a northern university in the unpropitious days of the Commonwealth, while in the later nineteenth century, when so many provincial universities were coming to birth, its moneyed leaders represented in the main the fine, but limited, Quaker tradition of zeal for school-education and adult 'self-improvement'. It may now be questioned whether, even if the necessarily astronomical funds were forthcoming, there exists a present demand for a fourth university in Yorkshire.[4] On the other hand, an institute of post-graduate calibre has already emerged from the efforts of the York Civic Trust. The diocese and the city possess between them our finest collection of historical documents outside London and the Trust has already organised at St. Anthony's Hall a centre for archive-study which may soon develop into something like a Northern Institute of Historical Research.[5] The Victorian ecclesiastical and county circles tended to a certain cultural stodginess, but now, besides its old Theatre Royal, York has a most lively Gallery, active historical societies and good concerts. Future observers may well take the Festival of Britain year as a landmark in its history. That year contained first and foremost the infinitely moving revival of the old Mystery Plays; it saw also the restoration and re-opening of the splendid Georgian Assembly Rooms,[6] where Sterne once ogled Kitty Fourmantelle; it provided a vigorous cosmetic treatment for the battered faces of old buildings and left the city looking lovelier than ever before.

In rough and ready simile, York may be regarded as a series of Chinese boxes fitting one inside the other. The outermost, a ring of ex-villages, mingled with the 'Strays' or grasslands preserved from time immemorial and including the Knavesmire and Racecourse. Embedded in this layer are the chocolate factories, the newer dormitories for railwaymen and artisans, the maze of marshalling yards to the west and the various military barracks. Inside this box lie the older suburbs, to which the genteeler sort of citizens retired during the last century; in the neighbourhood of the Mount you may yet see a few survivors peeping out of their chinks on Sunday afternoons. Still further inward, a complete circle of gated walls encloses the medieval city, one of great extent for its age, a city retaining twenty of its ancient churches, its Guildhall (this a war casualty, being rebuilt) and Merchant Adventurers' Hall, its Castle Keep, its King's Manor, its unkempt and seething mass of brick houses ranged around the enormous bulk of the Minster. And in the northern angle of this enclosure, especially in the grounds of St. Mary's Abbey, one may trace a settlement yet more central and far more ancient, since here the stretches of Roman wall and the Multangular Tower demarcate a city more than twice as distant in time from the creation of the Minster as this latter event from ourselves.

Of all these successive rings of occupation, it is the image of the medieval city which the name of York most often evokes; indeed it might prove hard to find outside Florence a square mile of streets more heavily laden with the earlier history of its people. Nevertheless, for every visitor who spares the three or four days necessary to develop even a nodding acquaintance with York, there must come a hundred racing across from the Station to see the Minster, between trains. Now the Minster belongs to the whole Northern Province; it is not York any more than the railway station is York; it is even less York than King's College Chapel is Cambridge. The city's true spirit must be sought in its civic buildings, its old streets and carved shop-fronts, its inns, gardens, turreted walls and forsaken corners, above all in its wonderful little parish churches which linked the hard heads of its old townsmen with the unseen and mythical worlds of their creed.

As for this Minster, I cannot remember the time when I did not know it after a fashion – did that knowledge only provoke a desire to climb on its tombs and play hide-andseek in its porches – yet always and unlike its compeers it has continued to grow bigger, grander, less approachable as the years passed. It is basic and institutional like some immortal great-aunt of our childhood; you may scarcely imagine the North without it, yet in place of mere pleasure and affection it forever nudges that questioning and curious demon at the back of the mind, the demon which makes odious measurements and comparisons, feeds on facts rather than beauty. Unity and grandeur the Minster possesses, but neither the organic unity of Lincoln with its climax in the Angel Choir, nor that grandeur which seems to grow from the rock at Durham. It has the most extensive and splendid galaxy of glass in the world, yet even in York itself the glass of at least three parish churches yields an infinitely warmer sense of intimacy with that generation of artists. And at the risk of pygmy-like impiety and ingratitude, I must record a merely personal impression that York has combined unity with vast proportions only at the expense of structural originality, of grace and variety in its detailed planning. Conceived on truly symphonic lines, it contains too many arid passages, too much mechanical and hastily elaborated orchestration. In the over-short nave the window traceries are monotonously reproduced; the famous West Front is covered with tiresome Perpendicular panelwork; the South Transept seems one of the least coordinated conceptions of its size in our cathedral architecture; the main roofs are flattened and wooden; the colossal central tower is not quite lofty enough to dominate, like that of Canterbury, the overall contour.

From such school-masterly strictures – so magisterial and self-confident a building cannot but produce this reflex in the overwhelmed beholder – we must clearly except the Early English North Transept, which, with its 'Five Sisters' window and the Chapterhouse in the background, forms by any canons of taste a most splendid and satisfying exterior. Upon the inward features of the Minster I dare not embark; for all who love our northern past, they are at once a treatise, a museum, and a delight. And that little building tucked in beside the South Door is the Diocesan Registry, where, like many other historians, I have spent laborious weeks transcribing the manuscript records of the diocese, transcribing them alongside the present diocesan officials, whose work preserves a marvellous continuity with that of my long-dead scribes. Nowhere more than in musty cathedral record rooms, not even in Duke Humphrey's Library at Oxford, may a scholar feel so integral a part of the ages which compiled these enormous theological summaries of stone.

The city churches, together the very quintessence of York, display a whole range of highly individual personalities quite defying brief analyses. The most outwardly impressive is All Saints Pavement, with its high open lantern, once holding the lamp which allegedly guided travellers toward York from the dark glades of Galtres Forest outside the northern walls. The most venerable is St. Mary's Castlegate, with its eleventh-century dedication-stone and complex structural history. Holy Trinity Goodramgate, most quaint and lovable, has a mass of jostling box-pews and three choice painted windows at its east end. The centre of these shows a daringly unconventional depiction of the Holy Trinity in the form of three seated Kings, while in the south aisle a very Nordic St. Olaf holds his three legendary loaves. The legend? That a servant girl was ordered by her master to bake on St. Olaf's day instead of praying at the Saint's shrine, so the Saint in revenge changed the loaves to stones and smote the impious master with blindness.

Such was the magic-anecdote mentality, the debased side of the religion professed by these late medieval people, who have given York the preponderant traits of its character. The solid and practical obverse of their minds one may best envisage in the Merchant Adventurers' Hall, now restored to its original state and testifying more eloquently than any building in England to our early commercial and overseas expansion.

Embedded amid the dark riverside lanes and warehouses lies the fairest jewel of old York, the church of All Saints North Street, which among the small churches of Christendom has no superior for painted windows. One is a contemporary tragic-strip illustration of a poem, *The Last Fifteen Days of the World*, until recently ascribed to the fourteenth-century Yorkshire mystic Richard Rolle, the surviving manuscripts of whose works prove him to have been a best-seller of the late medieval North. This window includes couplets extracted from the poem and sometimes amended by the designers to suit their space. On the seventh day, when the buildings fall, I much prefer their

> The seven day howses mon fall,
> Castels and towres and ilka wall.

to the original

> And grete castels and towres with alle.

And the modern spectator, when he comes to the eleventh day – a lull from the celestial air-bombardment – may well be pardoned a sense of recent reminiscence:

> The XI day sall men come owte
> Of ther holes and wende abowte.

Nevertheless, the dead rise, the stars fall from heaven,

> The XIII all that lives than
> Sall dy bathe childe, man and woman

and on the fifteenth day we see the whole terrestrial experiment atomised in lurid flames. At this prophecy, which, incidentally, remained current as late as a sermon of Jeremy Taylor, I once used to sneer as ludicrously unscientific! Nowadays, awaiting the outcome with more serious attention, we may at least enjoy a window which combines literary appeal with childlike treatment in a manner almost unparalleled in old glass. Its neighbour depicting the Corporal Acts of Mercy shows a painter of far more tender and poetic feeling, while the fragmentary east window of this aisle has that strangely jewel-like and compelling quality denied to all anecdotal themes. Only a dozen generations of flesh and blood separate us from these ancestors, yet when we have exhausted pages of cold print we often miss their warm comradeship, that evanescent sense of intimacy which comes all too rarely in a busy lifetime. One who would often feel the touch of a vanished hand on his shoulder would do well to pass an occasional hour alone in this dim-lit place.

York contained several monastic houses, one of them the wealthiest in all the North. This was the Abbey of St. Mary, the pathetic ruins of which stand in the grounds of the Yorkshire Philosophical Society on the north bank of the Ouse. An effort of imagination, stimulated by old prints, may suffice to re-create in mind this great lofty-towered church, three-quarters the length of the Minster and, judging by these Early English remains, far lovelier. St. Mary's, lying outside the city walls, protected itself against rebels and mobile Scottish raiders by the military precinct-wall still surrounding these gardens. The monks' guest house, further down the slope to the river, has been converted into a museum for Roman York. It houses much the finest collection taken from any one site of Roman Britain – pottery, glassware, fibulae, ear-rings, babies' feeding-bottles, votive tablets and, most movingly, the red-gold head of hair which once crowned some Romano-British lady and now lies on the post mortem table of the museum case.

Monk Bar, York, as it was in A. G. Dickens's childhood.
(Donald Sheldon)

The souls of cities respond even less easily than those of men to mere cataloguing; a hundred pages of it would never suffice to render the strong, unmistakable, yet wordelusive personality of York. As with that ancestral sense, you may feel it if you linger in the right places at the right times, perhaps on some spring evening when the sun is gilding this forest of red brick and white limestone. The dream descends as you walk along the northern parapet of the wall, when in the gardens of the canons' houses the stiff, gummy chestnut buds cluster between you and the Minster. It comes as you pause in the dusty, forgotten purlieus of Bishophill, a piano strumming in some melancholy terrace, the light dying on the bricks and tiles of the rose-red city. And even the exile may have his reminiscent dream, if he have the good fortune to possess a copy of Drake's *Eboracum*, that princely eighteenth-century forerunner of our great topographical works, which contains many an engraving of a York still more richly pinnacled and gabled, a York as yet little touched by those curious citizens and ecclesiastics who at irregular intervals herded together to destroy something of distinction and beauty. The fine Perpendicular church of St. Crux they pulled down in 1886 without even using the site. Their more recent exploit was the destruction of Christ Church, the little grey building which made delightful the junction of Shambles and Colliergate, now reduced to the ideal municipalised stretch of clean pavement with seats for pensioners.

As befits one of England's medieval streets famed in story and on calendar, the Shambles has survived this fate, though it is being subjected to a rather drastic restoration by the city authorities. In the process a number of houses are inevitably being rebuilt and – with almost as much inevitability – arty and crafty businesses are replacing most of the old butchers' shops which in one form or another

Window shopping in the much quieter Stonegate of A. G. Dickens's childhood. (Donald Sheldon).

have lined this street since before Domesday. But if in our time the Shambles becomes a Baltimore schoolmaam's idea of a medieval street, that will be nobody's fault except that of the medieval builder, who, poor fellow, failed to evolve the everlasting house. Just beyond the place where two exceptionally intrepid and long-armed people would just fail to shake hands across the street from the top storeys, there stands the house with the fantastically slanting front beam, where Margaret Clitherow lived. Submissive to her Protestant husband in all things save religion, she hid priests and heard masses until in 1586 the final blow fell. Then it was that this most famous of all York women was pressed to death near Ousebridge for refusing to plead against charges made under the penal laws. To-day she is officially beatified and the devout still go to venerate her little hand, preserved in St. Mary's Convent outside Micklegate Bar[7].

In these central areas you find the York which remains half late-medieval, half Georgian and Victorian, but not unnaturally, once you enter the houses, the last of these ages prevails. So writing, I suddenly recall those old maiden ladies with whom I used to lodge when working in York. They lived somewhere outside Bootham Bar in a gaunt brick Georgian house which badly needed painting, yet eyed its neighbours – mere parvenus of 1870 – with an air of marked suspicion and superiority. The elder lady, likewise somewhat angular and forbidding, concerned herself mainly with the management of inanimate objects, leaving matters of personal contact to her younger companion-piece, whose face was as benevolent as that of a pansy-flower. Both wore lace etceteras in the afternoons, black velvet throat-bands at all times. Paying guests they entertained in precise, well-drilled and démodé gentility. The teapots wore wondrously elaborate woollen jackets, but showed marked reluctance to pour; the knives had obviously been hard at work cutting bread and butter since Disraeli's premiership and were worn to shadows by their exertions. In the bedrooms many godly textcards

adorned the walls, while the secondary virtue of cleanliness was more dimly encouraged by large jugs of icy water.

One leaves the walled city by the Bars, all of which are different and all worth inspection. To avert misunderstanding in Mayfair, I should explain that in the Danelaw towns we do not necessarily crash gates or polish our elbows upon bars, since in addition to their commoner senses, these words signify respectively a street (Scandinavian *gatan*) and a 'city gate', Monkgate, for example, is the thoroughfare which leads from the dark arches of Monk Bar. In earlier times the Bars served both as barrack rooms and as exhibition stands for the heads of politicians who, in times of civil commotion, happened to back the losing party. Some incorporated houses, one of which still balances on pillars above Walmgate Bar, a delightful house I have always wanted to rent, if only in order to upset occasional jugs of cold tea over rich motorists who have just 'done' the Minster in ten minutes on their way down from the grand hotels and grouse-pogroms of the Highlands.

Beyond York the Vale extends northward through Easingwold, Thirsk and Northallerton to the valley of the Tees. Its central and most pleasing lands hence lie outside our purview; presumptuously but not altogether unjustly, the historian of Easingwold has called his book *Vallis Eboracensis*. Meanwhile the boundary of the East Riding turns east from York and across to the Derwent at Stamford Bridge, thence following the river into its upper courses in the Vale of Pickering.

Stamford Bridge will not long detain any save students of old battles – it consists of a cluster of houses on the river, an old mill, a weir and a mill-pool, around them miles of quiet wooded meadows. As for the battle, like most events of 1066 it has engaged the litigious faculties of our more tiresome historians, who have wrangled pedantically over every word of Harold Hardrada's Saga and Henry of Huntingdon –scribes compared with whom any bright American journalist, intent on stultifying his allies long after a campaign, is doubtless a paragon of factual accuracy! In one particular we are safe – in our refusal to attach undue reverence to the present bridge, which was built as late as 1727. The old Roman road actually crossed the Derwent by a wooden bridge well above this point, and here it was that a Norwegian disciple of Horatius held back our English host single-handed, until a regrettably unsportsmanlike Englishman took a boat and spitted him from beneath through the planks. I doubt whether even Professor Freeman, who wrote the classical account of this odd campaign, could have explained why the Norwegian engineers failed to use the respite to accomplish a bridge demolition, for such would at least have prevented the Englishmen from swarming over and giving Hardrada the seven feet of earth promised him by our Harold. But the Vikings, as archaeologists have shown, were enthusiastically

devoted to games of chance and also, no doubt, they had a keen eye to the next crop of war-songs, for Hardrada, the greatest of them all, was busy composing one on the eve of the battle itself. Lest, however, we should credit them with uniformly quixotic behaviour, we have been left their own evidence concerning the Norwegian Styrcar, who escaped from the carnage of Stamford clad in a shirt and armed only with a helm and a sword. Presently he fell in with a prosperous East Riding farmer and the *Heimskringla* recounts a conversation which ended with the farmer recognising Styrcar's Norse speech and Styrcar cutting off the farmer's head and relieving him of his fur-lined jacket, a welcome acquisition on that cold and windy evening.

From Stamford Bridge one may conveniently

Stamford Bridge Railway Viaduct (1846-7).
(JDL)

explore that most delightful and unspoiled north-western corner of the Riding which lies between the escarpment and the Derwent. Since the sale of Temple Newsam, Garrowby has been the chief residence of the Earl of Halifax, who, in a delightful and all-too-brief preface to Shepherd's *History of Kirby Underdale*, describes the pleasures of his boyhood at this ancestral seat.[8] A favourite among this group of villages is Langton, with its snug cottages along a grassy street, and its hall, which has lately made an ideal setting for a preparatory school. The annual prize giving here is preceded by a typically English, but very moving, service in the tiny village church, where the boys and their visiting parents sing and pray together. The present writer was recently privileged to attend this function and thereafter, in trying to say Something Improving, felt more inspired and far less like Bertie Wooster (on a similar but less ennobling occasion) than he had feared.

On Langton Wold, the chalk plateau north of the village, stretches the renowned training-course for racehorses and it is at this point that we enter the highly equestrian society of Malton. This latter place has its own sporting literature which a non-racegoer could not attempt to emulate. In any case, Malton itself lies across the Derwent and so in the North Riding.

Westward of these places and about four miles above Stamford Bridge begins the gorge of the Derwent, the point where we suddenly find the prosaic river encircled by a luxurious, undulating garden of countryside. 'Gorge' is indeed a word too strong, too suggestive of romantic eminences and torrents, but these theatres built of gentle banks and cool, clustering woods need fear no dramatic comparisons. They provide above all a signal instance of happy co-operation between man and nature, not least across on the North Riding bank, where Vanburgh's great Castle Howard amid its parks and plantations leads into a whole world of delight – the world of Sheriff Hutton, Helmsley, Byland and Rievaulx. I confess, were I petty kinglet of the East Riding, I should forever intrigue to annex this enchanting frontier-province, forever plead its cultural and landscape affinities to my own domains. Yet pending this act of aggrandisement, I might at least take pride in the firm tenure of Kirkham Priory.

This sole important monastic ruin in the East Riding, delightful both in situation and in the quality of its architectural remains, has been admirably excavated and stagemanaged by the Office of Works[9], which often contrives to please the antiquarian without too grossly offending the artist. Here, of course, I think primarily of us old-fashioned sketchers and dabblers, who like our ruins fuzzy and overgrown rather than functional and polished like steam-engines. Certainly with the aid of a theatrical, swooping cavalcade of passionate clouds, the great Turner could still make something of Kirkham. It stands just inside the fairest loop of the Derwent amid woods which even the railroad, so needlessly hugging the river, has not availed to pollute. It was once an important house of Austin Canons, founded along with Rievaulx about 1122 by the Norman baron Walter Espec, and, according to the popular but questionable legend, in memory of a son killed near this spot by a fall from his horse. The original Norman church, cloister and chapterhouse underwent careful medievalisation from the thirteenth century onwards, but had not been completed by the leisurely canons at the Dissolution three centuries later.

Of the surviving portions, the gatehouse remains the outstanding feature. Its arches now spring almost directly from the earth and above them on its outer face are ranged very recognisably the arms of Clare, Plantagenet, Ros, Vaux, Espec and Greystoke, the mighty families which patronised the house in the age when feudalism and monasticism were the twin pillars of European society. In the cloisters even the non-expert will at once identify what my admirable guidebook calls – with more accuracy than humour – 'the exquisite Geometrical *Lavatorium* (six basins), probably the loveliest remaining example of its kind in England'. Laugh while you may, yet ask whether, when great Selfridges is down, when Marble Arch forms two trunkless – and most ungraceful – legs of stone, when Oxford Street has joined the topless towers of Ilium, ask whether some searcher will describe in glowing superlatives the exquisite chromium-fitted *Lavatoria* of the First Atomic Era? I fancy not, though this journey up the flat vale, through the old City and thence to these remote and sylvan lawns of Kirkham would be amply rewarded by so fruitful, so sobering a reflexion. Yet in the last resort, this is again a place for magic rather than for moralising, a place where the wind-woven multitude of plants and trees chant their triumphs with a million green tongues, where the river flows re-silvered as from the slopes of Helicon, where the laurel-crowned hills cluster about like gods endowed with eternal youth and gazing down unmoved on the wasting heraldry, the stonework of mortal men. Always coming to Kirkham with the *pince-nez* of the archaeologist firmly fixed on my nose, I have never tried to write verses there, but the place has a purity of atmosphere conducive enough to poetry – the passion-spent purity of long dead thoughts and hands, the living purity of nature, ever newly emergent, ever freed from the memory of decay by the sweet, oblivious draught of Spring.

FOOTNOTES
1 Philip Saltmarshe, the last of the family, died in 1970.
2 The most famous family connection of the Babthorpes was Mary Ward, founder of the Institute of the Blessed Virgin Mary.
3 Local government changes have taken Selby into North Yorkshire.
4 York University was opened in 1963 and is now regarded as one of the country's leading universities.
5 The Borthwick Institute of Historical Research, University of York, incorporating Diocesan records, was opened in St. Anthony's Hall, Peasholme Green, 1953.
6 The Assembly Rooms were re-opened in 1951 with a grand Georgian Ball. After extensive reconstruction they were opened regularly to the public in 1994.
7 The relic of St. Margaret Clitherow (canonised in 1970) is kept in the Convent chapel. Access is through the Bar Convent Museum, Blossom Street, opened in 1987.
8 In his later autobiography, *Fullness of Days*, (1957), the late Earl of Halifax also wrote vividly of his childhood memories of Garrowby.
9 Kirkham Priory is now maintained by English Heritage.

Hills and the sea

A relief model of the Yorkshire Wolds somewhat resembles a thin segment pulled from an orange and laid flat upon a plate. The north point of this crescent is Flamborough Head; the south reaches the bank of the Humber near Ferriby. The segment's thicker and outer edge represents the bluff escarpment facing westward to the levels of York and northward to the Vale of Pickering; its thin inner edge shows the land falling gently into the plain of Holderness. And the odious traveller who measures a landscape by the height of its main peaks will find little to excite him in East Yorkshire; only near Wilton Beacon in the centre of the escarpment do the Wolds exceed a height of eight hundred feet. Nor do we welcome the companionship of those other critics who, misled by similar geological features, insist at every turn upon comparing this chalk range with the Sussex Downs or with the great white-bodied deserts of Wiltshire. The swelling contours of Southern England, which Huxley thought so suggestive of mutton and of pleasantness, are not precisely reproduced in the Yorkshire chalk, which belongs to a harder type partaking of limestone characteristics and weathering into somewhat abrupter reliefs. Yet at no great distance northward, escarpments decidedly bolder still are assumed by the hard calcareous grit of Oliver's Mount and the Nabs near Scarborough. And such geological distinctions apart, we must also recall that the personality of our Wolds has also developed in stimulating companionship with man, who has revealed depths and refinements which poor unaided Nature could never have deemed herself to possess. As for the components of that grown personality – a gentle, gay and adorable thing it is – a mere word-monger can at best hope to reveal them slowly and by implication. I say gentle and gay, thinking of ten months in twelve and momentarily forgetting the dead of winter, when our unfettered east wind can, more often and more cruelly than anywhere in England, pile gigantic snowdrifts, marooning the villages and starving the sheep.

The Wolds must be seen largely on foot; their intimate places are not quickly accessible from the motor-roads, while the roughness and sudden undulations of the lesser tracks harden the muscles of the cyclist only at the price of withering his spirit. Better to abandon transport at some strategic point and return to it after a circular walk; alternatively you may marry ordnance map with timetable, so planning itineraries between the several convenient 'bus routes and railway stations.[1] Yet if this latter project commends itself, let your time-margins be handsome, for our miles are proverbially long in Yorkshire and nowhere longer than around these sinuous waves of chalk. In the pages which follow we pursue no such detailed plans, but rather wander in imagination along the high crescent from south to north, from the sour, infertile carr-lands of Humberside to the immense cliffs of Flamborough, where the hills on their eastward march fall at last with precipitate grandeur into the sea.

Our line of escape, woldward, from the monotonous suburbs of Hull lies over these carrs through Cottingham, which Leland calls 'a great uplandisch town'. His epithet retains a certain propriety even in modern parlance, for the place, while boasting itself the biggest village in England, has indeed always been more of a market town than a village. It has a very large church, a central square complete with council-offices, a cross-roads with traffic lights, a long shopping street, an annual feast, a fine horse show and a marked communal sense which is unmistakably urban as well as suburban. That it has long betrayed signs of suburbanity one can scarcely deny, for even in Victorian times it attracted the more substantial merchants and industrialists of Hull, sidewhiskers, gold Alberts, family barouches and all. Their villas are still in most cases occupied by their spiritual and economic successors, though one at least of the merely spiritual type is left anxiously wondering how long his ostrich-like addiction to the last century will survive modern economic pressures. Some indeed of these edifices, including Lord Nunburnholme's business *pied à terre* and the old family home of the novelist Winifred Holtby, have recently bowed to the inevitable and have in fact met a far happier fate than might have been anticipated.[2] It so happens that the University of Hull has adopted Cottingham as its residential quarter, purchasing and adapting several of these roomier houses as halls of residence. Consequently, during term-time, the presence of several hundred bescarved young persons from all parts of England – not to mention most parts of the Colonial Empire – makes Cottingham something of a *Quartier Latin*, or at any rate as near one as anything you are likely to see in the East Riding. And amid such high-flown academic comparisons, we may claim that, though our Hallgate has not the grand sweep of Oxford High Street, it can at least show a St. Mary's which would bear serious comparison with the one in that famous thoroughfare by the Isis. Its nave belongs to the East Riding School of Flamboyant architecture (*c.*1340), a style prophetic of later Continental developments, one exemplified also in Holy Trinity, Hull, and in the collegiate churches of Beverley and Howden. The massive central tower has an external stair turret and, in order to give the whole structure a more balanced aspect, the cunning builder has divided the main face of the tower into two very unequal panels and put a much narrower window next to the turret. This odd feature passes unobserved even by ancient natives, who (*crede experto*) will freely wager half-crowns that such is not the case. The light and roomy chancel was built somewhat later by Canon Nicholas of Louth; it contains a very remarkable portrait-brass lauding his good works: *Famelicos pavit, rixantes pacificavit, nudos armavit.*[3]

North of the town, still on the flat plain, lies the market gardening area, the extreme fertility of which is said to result from a centuries-long deposit of night-soil from Hull. The isolated brick houses and small, well-tended fields remind one forcibly of the Lincolnshire fens and, perhaps still more forcibly, of the Netherlands. In fact a number of the most progressive growers are Dutchmen, who brought over their advanced techniques and first showed us how to cover the fields with glass.

The first gentle slopes of the Wold begin on the western edge of this spreading township and on the way toward them one may inspect a scheduled historical monument oddly unknown to the vast bulk of the inhabitants. This is the half-timbered manor house which lies down a lane toward the west end of Hallgate.[4] From a point near the house it is easy to trace the immense *enceinte* of earthworks which surrounded a once imposing medieval residence where the Stutevilles and the Wakes successively held court.

Just beyond Cottingham the high sails of Skidby Mill form a far-seen landmark and crown the first low ridge of the Wolds. Thence one soon reaches Little Weighton, with its characteristic street of brick cottages, and Rowley, which appears at first glimpse to consist of an isolated church and farmhouse in a park. Something of this 'deserted village' air it owes to the fact that its vicar, Ezekiel Rogers, a Puritan persecuted by Archbishop Laud for denouncing the *Book of Sports*, emigrated in 1638 with twenty substantial families of his flock and founded Rowley, Massachusetts. Past nearby Riplingham, the dale of Brantingham leads down the western escarpment to the level Vale. Here you should emphatically abandon the road and scramble to the top of the dale's northern shoulder, whence there opens a far prospect of the plain and the silver crescent of Humber. Never is this place more attractive than on some cool day in early summer, when you will be tempted to lie amid the gorse and cowslips half the afternoon, watching the sleepy sun-patches gilding the far river, soothed by the march of the clouds yet kept awake by the fresh flow of the still unbroken west wind. Across your middle ground the Roman road runs down from York; it is now reaching the point where generations of legionaries were ferried across the river on their way to and from the pacific southern province of Britain.

Near this ferry and now just north of Brough railway station, lay the Roman walled town of Petuaria. That a place of this name existed in Yorkshire was known from the *Antonine Iter*, but its whereabouts was disputed for centuries until the excavators of 1937, on the very day they were closing the season's work, unearthed an inscription which once for all fixed the site at Brough. The inscription recorded the erection of a stone theatrical stage by Marcus Ulpius Januarius, aedile of the town of Petuaria during the reign of Antoninus Pius (138-161 A.D.). During this prosperous second century Petuaria received its stone walls and, though it continued to be occupied until the very end of the Roman period, it grew no larger. We are still intermittently excavating portions of the twelve-acre site as opportunities arise and even the present writer has been known to wield a symbolic and ineffective spade. Further upstream lies Broomfleet, once a sequestered island, its sedgy banks still the haunt of wild geese. Round the mass of Wold to the right, South Cave with its old coaching inn, the Fox and Coney, typifies our larger villages and provides the obvious base for exploring the hills this side of the Market Weighton Gap.

Around Newbald and High Hunsley is revealed the sober, engaging charm of the lower Wolds,

with their little gorsewrapped dells and gulleys, their graceful skylines, ever changing because seldom far from the eye, their white roads bounding upward between the pale, chalk-laden fields. White is the keynote of the landscape and, if the Wold is a Symphony in White Major, these southern hills are its Slow Movement. As to their essentially major key, the casual wanderer in spring or summer will need little reassurance, for these are places where a man finds it easy to be solitary; unlike the great fells and moors of the other Ridings they hold no yearning, no wild regret, no thoughts too deep for tears.

Hereabouts the lazier antiquarian may spend a quiet day untorn by twinges of conscience, that is, if he but visit North Newbald, which, with the conceivable exception of Kirkburn near Driffield, has the finest

Blacktoft.
(JDL)

1. *Howden Minster: the chapter house*

2. *Beneath the Ouse Bridge, M62* (JG)

Norman church in East Yorkshire. To the rugged Norman belongs the high-windowed nave, the tower-arches, the superb south doorway with its surmounting vesica and Christ in Majesty. Within, we find an ornate Early English font, a chest with medieval ironwork and a long inscription to Sir Philip Monckton, a boastful Royalist hero buried here in 1678. In this interior the later ages are nevertheless overshadowed by a sombre Norman atmosphere, the devout spirit of an age swathed in the chain-mails of war and faith, when the earnest, fiery, miracle-haunted minds of these northern men bowed before mysteries half comprehended through the dimness of their tunnels of stone. Yet several centuries earlier the missionary St. Augustine is said to have converted the heathen of these parts, and if you turn southward across the fields from the two roads which bridge the Wold near Hunsley, you will find jutting from the hillside an entirely natural outcrop of rock called from time immemorial St. Austin's Stone. Whatever the reliability of the tradition, it is easy to imagine, standing aloft on the stone, the crowd of barbarians gathered in this grassy arena and awaiting open-mouthed the spell of the miracle-man in the white robe.

A much remoter past has, however, been revealed in this area and most vividly by the wonderful chariot-burials discovered on Arras Wold. These superbly accoutred warriors, who went to battle upon iron-tyred chariots, probably came from northern France about the middle of the third century before Christ. Ptolemy calls them the Parisi and it is clear that even during the Roman period their tribal organisation, centred upon Petuaria, remained distinct from that of the greater tribe of the Brigantes, who occupied the whole of the Pennine area. The reputation of our East Yorkshire Parisians has been somewhat undeservedly exceeded by that of their poor stay-at-home relatives, who gave their name to the French capital and so gained an easy place on the page of history by sheer lack of enterprise.

Two miles past Newbald and likewise at the foot of the hills lies Sancton with its octagonal church tower and its old parish register containing the entry: 'Monday, June 23rd, 1788. The Rev. John Wesley, M.A., preached here at 9 o'clock in the morning, at the age of 85, after having preached twice in the High Church at Hull the preceding day; and went from hence to preach at Weighton at eleven, at Pocklington at two; and at York in the evening of this day (4 times).' So inaugurated, the Methodist tradition of these Wolds soon outran the half-Anglican modes of the Wesleys, stole a march on the then easygoing clergy of the Established Church, traversed a heroic age of wandering, egg-pelted preachers and finally created these scores of forlorn, angular, Primitive Methodist chapels which, to all save the most historically-minded observer, disfigure even our smaller East Riding villages. And despite a real revival of Church life, Methodist religious forms continue a wide appeal in these rural parts, for they link easily enough with the plain-spoken radicalism of the Yorkshireman, with his suspicion of verbal elegance, with that emotionalism so often lurking below his hard-headed and matter-of-fact exterior. The Methodist preachers conquered the country in the vernacular; as one was heard to remark, 'There's nowt like a bit o' plain speakin' to wakken 'em up.'

A short walk westward from Sancton leads to Houghton Hall, where the park, easily accessible but little known, is perhaps the most charming of a whole row along the fringes of the Wolds. The view across the lake towards the old house has a timeless quality, in its frame of enormous trees. Any amateur of eighteenth-century family portraiture will know what I mean when I call it the perfect background for a group by Arthur Devis.

Sancton is famed in archaeological circles for its remarkable Anglo-Saxon urn-field, one of several along the Roman road toward York. These ugly black urns, rudely ornamented by knobs and patterns made by stick-ends, are the earliest relics of our squalid pagan ancestors. They frequently come to light in East Yorkshire and they even lie, giving an odd sense of continuity, amid the Roman cemeteries outside the walls of York. A few days after originally penning these words, I saw countless fragments of them scattered over a ploughed field on Sancton Wold and was rewarded for lingering by the usual soaking downpour which accompanies a casual archaeological ramble in the more shelterless expanses of East Yorkshire. Such urns may be inspected under far more comfortable circumstances in the Yorkshire Museum at York or in the almost equally noteworthy Mortimer Museum in Hull.[5] They are tantalising objects with exact counterparts in Hanover, Frisia and Jutland, the Continental homes of the English; if we could only establish their typology and elaborate an even approximate system of dating, we should be well on our way toward filling the most infuriating gap in English history – the fifth and sixth centuries.

At the point where the Roman road passes the east-to-west gap through the Wolds lies Market Weighton, the very platonic idea of a pleasant, humdrum little market town. Its last exciting event was the death in 1820 of its famous native, William Bradley, who in those days of grossly unplanned nutrition attained seven feet nine inches, weighed over 27 stones and very deservedly made a fortune in the man-mountain show-business. Yet the profound musings suggested by so portentous a natural prodigy we may well transfer to the adjacent village of Goodmanham, which happens to be among the most ancient and fascinating religious sites of the North. Its fame derives from that passage in Bede's *Ecclesiastical History* which describes the conversion of King Edwin of Northumbria (A.D. 626) by the great missionary, Paulinus. Along with Edwin, his pagan high priest, Coifi, threw off the old superstition, begged the King for arms and a stallion, rode lance in hand toward his temple and did not rest till he had smashed its idols and burnt it to the ground. 'This one-time place of idols,' says our Venerable Bede, 'is called today

Godmundingaham, where the priest himself, inspired by the true God, polluted and destroyed those very altars he had once consecrated.' The present church, probably occupying this same heathen site, contains two of the most remarkable baptismal fonts in the North. One is plain and perhaps of Saxon antiquity, a likelihood which did not spare it many years of use as a horse trough. The other, lovely and sophisticated, shows how Perpendicular carving continued in these parts into the mid-Tudor period, for its inscription, which begins *wyhtowt baptysm no saIl man be saved*, goes on to record as one of its donors a certain Robert Clevyng, a cleric known to have died in 1565. Amid these little hills, as in so many regions of Yorkshire, one has no sense of following some sidetrack forsaken in its rusticity; rather are they, together with the Ile de France and The Plain of Lombardy, a very focus of all those Christian ages whose domination over our minds was threatened but yesterday.

Beyond the Gap, yet still close to the escarpment, lies Pocklington, a market town of similar stamp to Weighton, but distinguished by a finer church and by an ancient public school, now, after a dull nineteenth century, a large and very lively institution. In the reign of Henry VIII it was placed under the patronage of St. John's, Cambridge, which college has been since that period pre-eminent for its acres, advowsons and influence in the East Riding.

The most wooded and park-like stretch of the range can perhaps be viewed to best advantage by walking southward from Pocklington, through Kilnwick Percy with its prim eight-columned hall and round the contours of the Wold to Nunburnholme. Seen in August this is a land of great green-bosomed copses, of shining cornfields framed by rank hemlock, campion, herb robert, bellflower, a land of rich gardens set amid steep and shapely hills. Like vast ocean-rollers they circle about us, on their crests plantations, long, dark and mysterious as the ships of a warrior race. The bright cottages of Nunburnholme stand at the entrance to an embowered chalk valley traversed by

3.　　　　　　　　　　　*York Castle*　　　　　　　　　　(JG)

4.　　　　　　　　　　*The Shambles, York*

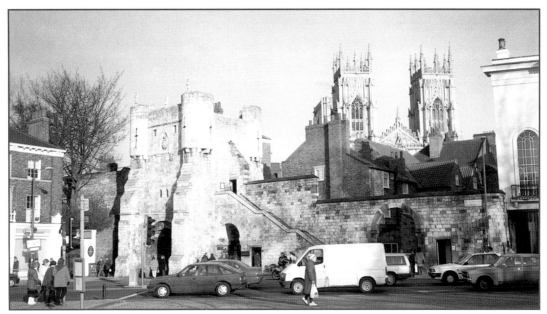

5.   *York: Bootham Bar*

6.   *South Cave*   (JDL)

Seaton Ross, showing the 19th-century Dial House Farm.   (JDL)

the Nuns' Walk, named, like the village itself, after a vanished Benedictine convent. Still more delightfully situated amid the woods on the left stood Warter Priory, the site of which has been excavated, revealing the whole ground plan, together with various monastic bric-à-brac and an abbot's incised effigy.[6] However hot the day, the resolute pedestrian will need to lunch without undue delay in the solitudes left by these dead religious communities and then ascend either the steep road, or the longer but more kindly track leading from the village across the brow of

Nunburnholme Wold. The tower of the church below was rebuilt as a memorial to Francis Orpen Morris, rector for forty years during the last century, who wrote a six-volume *History of British Birds* and played a major part in securing that beneficent legislation which protects our wild birds to-day. These wooded slopes have indeed gladdened the innocent heart of many an ornithologist, about eighty species of birds having been recognised within a short period inside the parish of Nunburnholme. The most spectacular air pageant occurs in autumn and winter, when great flocks of Pink-footed Geese, arriving on 24 September, fly each day with clockwork punctuality from their haunts along the Humber banks to scour these stubble-fields and return home at sunset.

Pressing on across the bare brow of the Wold, we descend into Londesborough, for me the beloved village of all Yorkshire, partly because invested with memories of long, carefree childhood visits, partly through its own pastoral loveliness and half-legendary associations. Here as a boy of seven, Henry Lord Clifford lay concealed among his mother's shepherds while his Yorkist enemies sought his life. Presently he was spirited away to even greater remoteness in Cumberland whence, on the accession of the friendly Tudor King in 1485, he emerged as a man of thirty unable to read or write. Erelong the Shepherd Lord turned studious astronomer, earning thereby a splendid poetic memorial, for it was on this theme that Wordsworth wrote his *Song at the Feast of Brougham Castle* and the finest passage in his *White Doe of Rylstone*. In the chancel of Londesborough church may still be seen the brass inscription to this Lord's mother, Margaret Vescy, who had brought the manor to the Cliffords by marriage and who lived to see the happy restitution of her son. On the failure of the Clifford line, these lands passed to the Earls of Burlington, the third of whom laid out this magnificent park, planted Londesborough Clump – said to be visible from Lincolnshire – and hollowed out a coomb in the Wold to improve its form. He was also a friend and patron of Pope, who, dedicating to him his *Use of Riches*, referred to this gargantuan landscape-gardening in the lines:

> Or helps the ambitious hill the heavens to
> scale
> Or scoops in circling theatres the vale.

This Earl, the builder of Burlington House, again befriended Garrick, a not infrequent visitor to Londesborough, where an avenue of elms was at last planted in his memory.

Here the parson, Brian Allott, asked the great actor to give him some hints on effective Bible-reading in church. Garrick agreed. Allott ascended the lectern and opened the Bible, but he was instantly told to repeat the operation and open it a second time, not as he would a day-book or ledger, but as if he felt it to be the very word of God.

From these Earls Londesborough passed to the Cavendishes, with the result that in 1819 the sixth Duke of Devonshire stupidly pulled down the old hall. Treading the empty green site and terrace which he left, we may still enjoy the splendid prospect across the park and its encircling high plantations. Small wonder that the destructive noblemen on revisiting this spot 'shed tears over the ruin he had wrought', though he ultimately consoled himself by selling the Londesborough lands for nearly half a million to George Hudson the Railway King.

During the railway boom of the century's middle years, this latter magnate, who had begun public life as a York draper and Lord Mayor, dominated the local scene. 'Mak all t'railways coom ti York,' he dictated in his broad native accent at a planning conference, and so they did, as we may witness to-day.[7] In like regal manner he routed this York-Market Weighton line to ensure his easy personal transit to his Londesborough estate, where at the end of the long avenue he enjoyed the amenity of a private station. And even though in his catastrophic fall he dragged down thousands of poorer speculators, Hudson scarcely belongs to the rogues' gallery of finance and in his heyday was a notable benefactor of his native city of York.

Upon a lower ridge some miles to the east rises the most striking human landmark of the whole Riding, the spire of South Dalton, planted like an enormous arrow in the breast of the Wold. This church, ornate and beautiful in its shining white stone, is one of the outstanding achievements of John L. Pearson, architect of Truro Cathedral, who deserves applause for refusing purist advocacy of a mere lifeless imitation of local styles in local stone. The Wolds do

7.   *East Yorkshire harvest: near Bishop Wilton*   (JDL)

8.   *Wilberfoss*   (JDL)

9. *An East Yorkshire seascape: Flamborough* (JG)

10. *Old Town, Bridlington* (JDL)

not indeed demand that everything should blend sentimentally, for their own aspect has been much changed by man; too mild to seek domination over him, they have yet a receptive faculty, which, accepting the works of his hand, creates harmonies from his stridencies. Dalton has been associated for many generations with the Hotham family, an early member of which we shall see defying King Charles at Hull. The present church accordingly contains a memorial, older than itself and carved in Italy, in honour of a Sir John Hotham who died in 1689. This most remarkable baroque monument in the East Riding comprises four life-sized female figures representing Truth (with mirror) Strength (with broken column) Justice (with sword) and Temperance (with water jugs). All these ladies kneel on one knee, robustly supporting on their shoulders a black slab and the recumbent figure of the knight in full armour. The connoisseur will note the sinuous realism with which these sculptors treated the lower limbs of their figures in a period long before a million stocking-advertisements had created the present standardised and tiresome anatomical ideal.

The highest Wolds one may best approach from the direction of Huggate, itself perhaps our most characteristic hill-village. Climbing steadily past the six parallel ancient dikes and the further entrenchment along the Driffield-York road, the pedestrian at last reaches Wilton Beacon and its rewarding vistas across the chequered woods, meadows and ploughlands in the Vale of York and, far to the right, over the wooded, winding gorge of the Derwent. Still more impressively, a point like Leavening Brow commands a view running through three quarters of a circle; southward the broad Vale sweeps from the Humber flats past York to the Howardian Hills and the gardens of Kirkham, breaks more decisively in the Pennine mountains far to the west and the high moorlands to the north. Hence, as from several other places along this western escarpment, York Minster looms into view, bulks

surprisingly large over so many miles, rides like a vast galleon with all sails set across the haze of the plains. All far views of York are more than dominated by the gigantic mother church; they tend to consist almost solely of its square-cut, three-towered profile. No hills rise close enough to reveal in full the clustering lesser beauties of our capital, to make it a silver-pinnacled city of Camelot, the city into which Oxford is still transformed from Elsfield or Boar's Hill.

From this point the Wold changes direction, starts its long eastward march to the sea and yields a further series of panoramas across the Vale of Pickering with its superficially pleasant, but ill-drained farms, behind which ranges the frontier of the limestone and the purple moor. Often as I have trodden their slopes, I confess I am no true native of these northern Wolds. Despite the last century's ploughs and foresters, I shall never find them as homely as I find the paths of Hunsley and Londesborough. They hold a spirit mysterious and elusive, a kinship with White Horse Hill and the Wiltshire Downs about the great prehistoric theatre of Avebury. The origin of this spell seems not far to seek. Countless primitive generations have lent all these places a strange air apparent not merely to the scholar but to any mind in tune with the fugitive, half-seen hints and hunches of a countryside. And no hills in England may claim precedence over our northern Wolds for their tangible relics of Early Man. Hence through millenia he descended at dawn to water his flocks at Acklam Springs or, further afield, to chase the deer and wild boar through Galtres Forest; at the end of the long day he returned to the crude meal, the working of intractable flint and bone, the sleep in the smoky hut upon these high bastions of chalk. He follows us the moment we leave the prosaic valley and the village hearths, follows mutely with his ditches, his barrows, his multitudinous flints disturbed in the fields by every downpour of rain. Whenever we reach the hilltops we walk in his land; well may we imagine his mockery as we fail, for all our vaunted historical imagination, to comprehend his manner of thought, to enter the mind in its red dawn when time and reason themselves flowed by laws slow and obscure.

With the Bronze Age we nevertheless begin to insinuate ourselves into his confidence. He has now, after all, become an honest weaver and an agriculturalist who grows wheat, keeps sheep and cattle. Moreover, he has, even in East Yorkshire, a religion, even if it can hardly keep pace with those of the Israelites and other more gifted Bronze Age peoples. The ornamentation of the chalk drum-idols found at Folkton coincides with roughly contemporary symbolism in the Aegean, in France, in Ireland and in Denmark. These signs point to the worship of a Mother Goddess, while at Kellythorpe near Driffield the hawk's head associated with a beaker-burial strongly indicates sun-worship. Ideas and techniques were now crossing Yorkshire *via* the Aire Gap, the York moraine and the Wolds, since these lay on a trade-route between prosperous gold-working Ireland, with its Mediterranean influences, and Scandinavia. This route is marked not merely by identical axes, but by cist-burials of markedly Irish type and again by several tree-trunk burials (of the food-vessel period, which succeeds that of the beakers) indicating intercourse with Jutland and Schleswig, where they are common. These Bronze-agers are the early Yorkshiremen I should most like to meet; I always imagine them as rather subtle and interesting creatures, compared with their Iron Age successors, the Parisi, whom we met at Arras Wold. Were these latter not, after all, rather brainless warriors in the worst Homeric tradition, rushing around in mobile armoured columns? And, when at last they met the forerunners of Rome (in the Mediterranean traders preceding the Legion) did they not wear somewhat puzzled expressions like those of Oxford rowing Blues who have strayed into a Bloomsbury party? I blush to publicise such private imaginings until I reflect that I am now in good company – they seem commonly accepted in a day when pre-Roman archaeology has become the seemliest of all the handmaids of poetry!

These crowding earthworks of the northern Wolds seldom admit of facile explanation; they seem to run everywhere and at all angles. Sometimes, as at Aldro on the outer corner of the escarpment, they enclose a small, clearly defined area, yet, taken as a whole, they spread too widely in time and type to fit the neat schemes of defence fabricated by over-imaginative, or rather unimaginative, theorists. Their complexity is the outcome of an occupation stretching from the remote age of the long barrows into historical times. Doubtless many on further investigation will prove to be village and town enclosures, others hollow roads, yet others field boundaries and animal compounds. Century after unchronicled century, men dwelt in their thousands upon these high grounds and where they dwelt they dug with a stubborn and timeless zeal. The two greatest of their works do in fact seem the most clearly defensive in character and both defend the Flamborough peninsula. The outer one, the Argam Dike, now extending for five miles from Reighton to Rudston, consists of three banks and two ditches, in all 35 yards wide. Much more impressive is the famous Danes' Dike, two and a half miles long and shutting off almost the whole headland from sea to sea. In places it still stands eighteen feet high with a western ditch some sixty feet in breadth; it contains flints of the mid-Bronze Age and was ostensibly constructed by the cape-dwellers of that era to guard their five square miles against the mainland tribes.

From medieval times until a century and a half ago, the greater part of the Wolds remained like the Berkshire and the Sussex Downs, a long green sheep-walk, untimbered and scarcely broken by the plough. Here and there a few thin fields of oats and barley yielded the only native grain, while vast areas, perhaps nearly ten thousand acres, were occupied by fenced rabbit warrens. In very large measure the repainting of this primitive agrarian picture may be ascribed to the imagination and assiduity of one

11.   *Rudston Monolith in All Saints churchyard*   (JG)

12.   *Hull Fair*   (JDL)

pioneering family, a family whose history remains virtually the history of the northern Wolds. Sir Christopher Sykes, who held his baronetcy between 1784 and 1801, planted fir, larch, ash and birch thickly and extensively; stimulated by the rising demand for wheaten bread, he made his people plough up the fields. Everywhere he grew hedgerows and built new roads with wide grazing verges for the use of the poor. His elder son, Mark, notable rather as gambler, art collector and bibliophile, died childless in 1823 and was succeeded by a brother, Sir Tatton Sykes. This latter, the legend, the institution and the epitome of our nineteenth-century East Riding, conducted his life as if time and failure did not exist. He married only at fifty, lived with superhuman vigour until over ninety, all the while planting, ploughing, hunting, boxing, stone-breaking, building schools, inventing bone-fertilisers and breeding the finest sheep and hunters in all England. Between him and his admiring tenants there existed a bond of unity reminiscent of the older feudal North. Indeed, when I think of this godlike squire, the idol of my own grandfather's boyhood and the saga of his old age, I feel half disposed to cast away this part of my manuscript and rewrite it simply as a life of the elder Sir Tatton Sykes.[8] Yet I will adhere to my plan, since with a topographer's low cunning I have already brought the reader near Sledmere, residence of the Sykes and capital of their wide domains.

It is situated on high ground, yet in a slight declivity hung about with great canopies of trees. At first sight the whole village seems to bristle with monuments erected at various times by the family. They include a well-proportioned 'Eleanor' cross, incorporating a later war memorial with curious brass portraits of the local dead. Less pleasant, in some measure intentionally ugly, is the Waggoners' Monument, designed by the late Sir Mark Sykes to commemorate a transport company which he personally raised from among the Woldsmen in 1914.[9]

Only five years later this brilliant orientalist, politician, soldier and traveller, very much the fine flower of his family, died while actually attending the Paris Peace Conference. On Garton Hill outside the village stands the enormous spire-monument to old Sir Tatton, and from its upper chamber the breathless climber gazes over sixteen miles of coastal plain. Beyond it lies a remote painted ocean. Yet the supreme attraction of Sledmere is a church which even the most cautious judge would place among the half-dozen loveliest modern village churches in England.[10] It stands inside the leafy park free of any churchyard-bounds, yet islanded in spring and early summer by a lake of flowers. The tower is old, the rest built of rose-tinted stone during the 'nineties from the designs of Temple Moore, that able reviver of the Decorated Style. Up a winding staircase you find a little study hung with tapestry and furnished with Mark Sykes's own favourite books: Dante, Milton, Bunyan, the *Imitation*, the Bible. This room which he loved forms his truest memorial.[11]

Sledmere church is but the gem of a whole series either rebuilt or restored by the younger Sir Tatton, son of the old baronet of that name and Sir Mark's father, who between the late 1860's and his death in 1913 – an age when money *was* money – spent nearly two million pounds on building[12]. Unconventional, shrewd, reserved, tongue-tied, disliking fashionable society, this fifth baronet was by no means the least remarkable of his dynasty. As a good judge will, he passed only his summers on the Wolds, where, according to my elders, he would daily set off walking, enveloped in numerous coloured waistcoats. These, as he became warmer, he would cast to the roadside one by one, leaving them to be collected by a footman, who followed him for this express purpose, yet at a respectful interval. The rest of the year he spent travelling in Europe, China, Russia, Japan and America. He would journey thousands of miles to see a cathedral; here at home he consummated the pioneering triumphs of his forbears by clothing these newly-won lands with a robe of churches and schools. His first and most prolific architect was Street, responsible for the Wold churches of Wansford, Thixendale, Fimber, Kirby Grindalythe, Helperthorpe, West Lutton and East Heslerton. Subsequently he employed Pearson, Temple Moore and Hodgson Fowler, the last to design Langtoft and Sherburn. All these places lie within easy reach of Sledmere, making the region a playground not only for students of the Bronze Age but also for those of Victorian Man, in his turn become a period-piece if not yet a mystery.

The last time I walked on these hills and gazed across the Derwent Woods, I confess I was recalling memories even more recent and mundane. Somewhere in that green valley I sought to recognise the strange village where I arrived on military business one dark, mid-war winter evening. The battery I was visiting had drawn up its guns and vehicles in the back streets and yards amid much flashing of lamps, barking of dogs and concourse of excited young women. Parties of men were being dismissed and preparing to 'get their feet under the tables' of the village. The officers had taken up their quarters in the public house – one of those shabby East Yorkshire hostelries, its interior covered with brown paint, photographs of horses, mirrors covered with broken enamel characters, amongst which those skilled in runes might decipher the spell-words BASS and WHITBREAD. A dispirited batman was attempting to cook a meal in the basement, where the oven had been out of action for twenty years. So encouraged, the guest had to ascend to the mess by a Tarzan-like feat of athletics, the staircase between the third and seventh steps being conspicuously absent. Up there sat four officers grimly discussing the prospects of a wash, since the water had been turned off, and of a cooked meal, in view of the shortage of fuel. A fire had just flickered to extinction in the antique grate. From time to time a woman, her face partially concealed by a black shawl, glowered in eerie silence through the open door at the unwelcome guests. It was one of those macabre evenings when the soldier simply puts up his mental shutters and breathes a prayer of thanks for the ready gift of sleep. Rising at dawn, I cut the mud from my boots, drove back furiously along the clean, snow-powdered contours of the Wolds and after a long spell amid foreign fields and places, completely and tantalisingly forgot even the name of that accursed village. Sometimes I try to dismiss the whole episode as a dream, or at least to persuade fellow-sufferers that rural Yorkshire in wartime gave but a poor foretaste of its delights in peace.

In particular our country inns, though often hard on the eye and primarily centres of village gossip and conviviality, are seldom reluctant to relieve the civil foreigner of his money. There, unless you usurp the seat of a 'regular' or indulge in supercilious ruderies about Yorkshire, you will normally be welcomed by the host and his clientèle as freely as anywhere in England. East Yorkshire countrymen are in fact not exceptionally clannish as countrymen go, though they may often seem insular and unduly county-patriotic. 'That's real Yorksheer,' one still hears as the most unequivocal praise which can be awarded. You may watch them come in from 'fotherin' oop pigs' only to start discussing cows' ailments, village deaths and amatory misdemeanours, but you will find this cloak of rural simplicity fall away when you venture on a business deal. Talkative and open-mouthed over small things, these men turn highly cautious 'when it cooms ti partin' wi brass'. When you get on terms of confidence you may find your public-house friends rather superstitious – though less so than their cousins in Cleveland – and a trifle morbidly inclined to discuss diseases and funerals. Nevertheless these last you will find in practice highly ambivalent functions, for 'viewing the body' is still frequently followed by a social reunion, lugubrious merely on the surface for those many guests not intimately attached to the deceased. On such occasions I have seen strictly teetotal Methodists accepting a glass of port, while the company eyed with unaffected interest the capacious apple pie and the noble ham on the sideboard. Indeed,

Flamborough churchyard.
(JDL)

The Old Lighthouse, Flamborough: 1764.
(JDL)

a 'ham funeral' used not long ago to be regarded as the *sine qua non* of a respectable transit from this world. And if our countryman proves stingy in business deals, he can, especially when, as he would put it, he has 'summered and wintered' you, become an extremely generous host. Nor is our local prowess limited to curing hams, for only a bigoted observer will fail to recognise the truth that authentic Yorkshire pudding seldom emerges outside the county of its origin. We expect our women to bake their own bread and cakes; we unashamedly like tea with beefsteak and chips, prefer cheese with apple pie and plenty of butter on rich currant cake. Our best meal is a sort of hybrid tea-dinner-supper between five and six in the afternoon, an unforgettable experience at any Yorkshire farmhouse as you sit round the table between the red fire and the high dresser with its shining rows of plates. And remember that eating with a Yorkshire farmer's wife is rather like drinking with a Russian – you are apt to give offence if you fail to partake with adequate enthusiasm. It would, of course, be highly improving to report that all these delights had now given place to a uniform and public-spirited austerity, but without recording my evidence, I will merely express a lingering doubt. As for the local character in general, it may not be fully assessed without reference to its dialect and mode of expression, matters I reserve for later mention. Meantime we cannot exclude from our Wold journey the cliff-scenery around Flamborough, since these famous precipices are but the defiant gestures of the chalk uplands to a sea which has heavily defeated the softer lands to the north and the south. The area deserves at the very least two strenuous days of exploration, one to follow the coast down from Filey, the other to survey Flamborough Head itself. The first of these places, its core a delightful old fishing town with many antique traditions and nooks, has unfortunately decked itself with the trappings of a seaside resort. I myself can just remember our holidays at Filey during the 1914 war,

when it had already reached the 'select' stage and when we received with shocked bourgeois incredulity the news of the bombardment of nearby Scarborough. To-day as then, Filey's most attractive walk lies along the Brig, the low promontory of oolitic rock whereon the breakers literally explode, looking in heavy weather not unlike the receiving end of an artillery barrage. Becalmed, it is a place of worn, tilted boulders, dark weed clusters, sea-tints shifting and iridescent, the lilt of gull wings across the enormous sky. A morning alone in these retreats can assume a strangely timeless quality, can arouse even that sort of quasi-spiritual experience one associates with bare mountain crests and desert places. This I have felt even more vividly in Thornwick Bay, a cove down on the Head itself, where the fortunate wanderer may happen to lie just as drastically severed from human contact by a narrow amphitheatre of chalk cliffs, one of which leaps up from the shore in the form of a great white arch like those near the Giants' Causeway. At his feet the waters seethe in victory, then sigh in retreat; he feels in each pebble and boulder a bare and bone-like quality; sun and air, shattering in their brilliance, dazzle and absorb his spirit.

What opposite extremes of experiences, what conflicting versions of happiness, are represented on the one hand by these solitudes and on the other by that socially beneficial and mass-minded holiday camp recently grown up south of Filey![13] Between this heavily invaded point and Flamborough Head – that is, through Speeton, Buckton and Bempton – stretches one of the noblest and loftiest cliffwalks in England. These merely conventional epithets I retain as befits a man with neither head nor enthusiasm for heights, who belongs in spirit to an earlier, pre-mountaineering age when such 'dizzy eminences' were accounted 'horrid'. The far greater heights experienced from an aircraft move me not at all, since the earth has then become a remote panorama, a mere cinema film so unreal as to seem incapable of springing up and dashing one into darkness. But this three-hundred foot wall, linking the eye with the white rocks and the foam, fills me with mingled challenge and repulsion, induces a tension in the leg-muscles and confronts me face to face with man's primeval and persistent foe, the force of gravity. Minds thus feebly constituted may nevertheless achieve a vicarious excitement by watching the egg-gatherers at work with their ropes and pulleys upon these cliffs. Like petals in a spring gale, the guillemots, the kittiwakes, the razorbills, the puffins scatter and turn about the abyss; they wail and chatter over their bereavement as the plunderers swing across the cliff face gathering in their blue eggs from ledge and cranny. And the watcher finds himself so describing this sport from the birds' viewpoint, the ways of men being so much more freakish and pointless.

Though the Danes' Dike which defends the peninsula had no relation with the Danes, a whole series of legends has gained this territory the name of Little Denmark. The Constables, for many centuries the great family at Flamborough, supposed their rent due to the King of Denmark and, by way of annual token, shot an arrow bearing a gold coin from the cliffs into the sea. The so-called Danish Tower, in all likelihood the last relic of the old Constable mansion, stands near the church, inside which an outstanding personality is commemorated by one of the most singular monuments in Yorkshire. Its long brass inscription relates how valiantly Sir Marmaduke Constable, then aged seventy, fought at Flodden:

> But now all these tryumphes ar passed and set
>   on syde.
> For all worldly joyes they wull not long
>   endure.
> They are sone passed and away dothe glyde,
> And who that puttith his trust in them I call
>   hym most unsure,
> For when deth strikith, he sparith no creature,
> Nor gevith no warnyng, but takith them by
>   one and one. . .

Below this lies a fragmentary 'cadaver', displaying with gruesome realism the dead man's heart – a *jeu d'esprit* thought to refer to the story that the old hero's heart was gnawed away by a toad he had inadvertently swallowed. Only sixteen years later, his son, Sir Robert Constable, was hanged over the gates of Hull for complicity in the Pilgrimage of Grace, that most crucial revolt against the 'advanced' policy of Henry VIII. This, incidentally, was the biggest independent political flutter of the East Riding, which for once gave the lead to the rest of the North. As for the great headland of Flamborough, placed athwart our main coastal shipping route, it has witnessed in bygone centuries more than one novelish maritime episode. Here a watcher one sultry August afternoon saw the resplendent French galleys bearing the young widowed Queen of Scots to her northern tragedy. Here, two hundred years later, the villagers enjoyed a grandstand view of that truly epic sea-fight between the American Paul Jones and the English Captain Pearson. All this while and even at the outset of the last century Flamborough was accounted among the most barbarous and insular places in England, strangers fearing to approach it unfriended and unannounced. Both the Flamborough area and the coast of Holderness boast a lurid history of smuggling gangs, though it seems permissible to doubt whether local life was ever in fact so romantically insecure as depicted in Oliver Onions' delightful novel *The Story of Ragged Robyn*. Reading those breathless, dream-like pages, one might wish – retrospectively at least – that truth had indeed outstripped fiction. And writing of East Yorkshire novels, one recalls that Flamborough life of the late eighteenth century has been ably re-created by an earlier storyteller, R. D. Blackmore, in his long novel *Mary Anerley*, which, if not in the same class as his masterpiece, contains some admirable scenes. I confess that at this stage I am no longer greatly stirred by the virtuous loves of Mary and the smuggler Robin Lyth, even though the latter was a real enough character to give his name to one of the Flamborough caves. Nevertheless these old novelists observed well and wrote incredibly well, when for once they forgot to moralise and excogitate poetic justice for their characters. In particular, Blackmore's thumbnail landscapes retain a lasting appeal, as when, for example, he speaks of the great rareness of undisturbed and flawless summer days at Flamborough: 'Often the air shines brightly there, and often the air broods hot with thunder; but the sun owes his brightness to the sweep of the wind, which sweeps away his warmth as well ; while on the other hand, the thunder clouds, like heavy smoke capping the headland, may oppress the air with heat, but are not of sweet summer's beauty.'

To-day many Flamburians still lead the life of a fishing community, a blue-jerseyed, sea-booted, brown-skinned and weather-beaten life, a hard life not truly sensed by the casual summer visitor who dawdles away one of those hot thundery afternoons at the North or the South Landing, watches the donkeys sleepily carry up the catch in their panniers. But on such a day your deepest delight is to circumnavigate the headland itself, to feel, once out of shelter, the unbroken rollers, thrice your boat's length, bear it onward with smooth, powerful gestures scarce concealing a hint of menace, a dormant caprice.

Our Wolds have sometimes been judged less than perfect because they lack streams and lakes, yet this want is more than compensated by their ever-present sense of the sea which is at once their aim, their affinity and their tomb. Here in the north the breath and air of the sea never fail, even when its surface lies invisible to the eye. You feel the sea alike in the billowing autumn fogs and the fierce blasts of March; most audibly of all does it breathe when the smokeless light of an early summer morning turns the world to jewels glittering in the wind. This I remember sensing when young, though as ever with youth, my vision of natural beauty was darkened by red images of tooth and claw.

FOOTNOTES

1 The 'convenient' bus and train services of 1954 have considerably declined over the past half-century.
2 Lord Nunburnholme's Bungalow is now Hull University's Cleminson Hall. Holtby House, the former home of the novelist, which became a hall of residence, has since been sold by the University.
3 He fed the hungry, calmed the quarrelsome, clothed the naked.
4 Cottingham's Manor House off Hallgate is described by Pevsner as 'one of the best surviving timber-framed farmhouses in the East Riding'.
5 The contents of the Maritime Museum in the City Hall were transferred to the Museum of Commerce and Transport in High Street and opened there in 1957. This museum has since been renamed the Hull and East Riding Museum.
6 Dickens is referring to the medieval monastery of Warter Priory. The mansion known as Warter Priory, which was aggrandised by C. H. Wilson, later ennobled as Lord Nunburnholme, was demolished in 1972.
7 The statement attributed to Hudson is now regarded as apocryphal. See A. J. Peacock and D. Joy, *George Hudson of York* (Dalesman Books, 1971). It is also doubted whether he ever lived at the Londesborough estate which he had purchased [See David Neave, *Londesborough: history of an East Yorkshire estate village* (Londesborough, 1977)].
8 Although Sir Tatton Sykes, the 4th baronet, was the hero of his fellow-countrymen, a very different picture of him emerges in an essay by his great-grandson, Christopher Sykes, *Four Studies in Loyalty* (1946, 1988 edn), which depicts him as a sadistic, tyrannical father.
9 The Waggoners Reserve was founded in 1913.
10 Dickens makes no mention of the superb Sledmere House, then entirely private but now open to the public.
11 The study in the church is no longer open.
12 The reputed £1½ million which Sir Tatton, the 5th baronet, spent on church restoration and building is an exaggeration resulting from an error copied by later writers. Professor Barbara English discovered that the correct figure of £150,000 (a much more realistic total of the sum needed for his projects) had been multiplied by the accidental addition of another nought.
13 Butlin's Holiday Camp, in its heyday when Dickens wrote, suffered from the growing popularity of Continental holidays and closed in 1983.

The third port

Allow me a gesture of contempt toward those exquisite literary topographers who, after rhapsodising over York and Beverley, either turn aside from Hull with open disgust or accord it but an agonised and grimacing page. True, amid its fish-manure and seed-crushing plants some strange, even disagreeable odours not infrequently arise. True, despite decades of active reform, it has too many acres of brick and slate, mouldering slumwards and crying loudly to Apollo for redress. True again, a fair proportion of its inhabitants might seem, on superficial acquaintance, as insular, hard-accented a company of Philistines a man would be likely to encounter upon a leisurely journey from Pimlico to Peebles. Heaven forbid we natives should wax too indignant over such charges, yet one who half perforce, half willingly, has spent most of his life elsewhere, cannot return to the old home without a sense of pride in its gallant past and its recent heroism, without many affectionate memories, without a confident belief that more satisfying modes of life, both physical and spiritual, will flower even from amid its unlovelier wastes. And neither the ill-fated efforts of town-planners nor the recent destructive rain of fire have sufficed to break our visible links with the past. Many of those buildings and scenes which made Hull something of a boy's paradise have emerged unscathed; the Old Town and harbour still bear witness to a mercantile history already resplendent in days of the Hanseatic League.

I take the inevitable point of departure to be our City Square,[1] the point where the heavily-battered modern meets the more intact Old Town. Previous to 1941 this square and its encircling streets consisted mainly of 'handsome' late Victorian and Edwardian edifices, of which the surviving City Hall and Dock Offices[2] provide favourable examples. These confront the more modern Ferens Art Gallery,[3] a charming Egypto-Corinthian affair which has also deservedly outlived several of its neighbours, and which, in place of the dull Edwardian canvasses I remember, now contains a discriminating collection of contemporary British paintings. In the centre of the square stands a statue of Queen Victoria, with Britannia somewhat nonchalantly reclining at her feet. I well remember how years ago this group suffered temporary removal

Queen Victoria Square, Hull: Maritime Museum right.
(JDL)

to permit the excavation of a labyrinthine catacomb of conveniences; then how, with a certain insensitivity vaguely reminiscent of *Clochemerle,* it was replaced in full command of the equivocal situation. In the east corner of the square there stood in those days the hundred-foot column supporting the figure of our great citizen William Wilberforce, who, clad in a toga and with emotions imperceptible at that altitude, surveyed the seething streets and docks around him. Yet this statue too I was privileged to see dismantled in its turn – and a grim product of the stonemason's yard it proved, at close quarters. Again ignominious was the occasion – the filling-in of that delightful eighteenth-century Queen's Dock, which had so long attracted a seething crowd of masts and funnels here into the very heart of the city, but was obviously too colourful to survive those drab, unhappy years. To-day you can see poor Wilberforce once more playing the pillar-saint, but now at the far end of the Queen's Gardens, which, with the projected museum and technical college, will by 1970 resemble the Champs Elysées more closely than at present[4]. What chances we missed when abolishing that dock! If we had to lose our ships, we might at least have gained a pleasure-lake similar to the Inner Alster in Hamburg, surrounded perhaps by cafés and music and little chestnut trees, crossed by the greyhound shapes and white wings of yachts and launches. Yet even then one knew how sadly our people lacked the instinct for elegance and visual seemliness, how slowly we were parting company with our otherwise splendid Victorian forbears, who vainly thought to scare the nymphs and satyrs from their cities by erecting statues of the Great Queen – and even of themselves!

Further back in time, before the digging of these old central docks, there stood at this same corner the Beverley Gate: from its safe eminence our governor, Sir John Hotham, conducted a courteous altercation with King

Charles I, to whom, at the very outset of the Civil Wars, he refused to yield this vital port. To-day there remains not a trace of the strong brick walls and their twenty-four towers which protected the two landward

Statue of Queen Victoria.
(JDL)

sides of the Old Town.[4] This last we enter between the crowded shops and coffee houses of Whitefriargate, admiring the lane called the Land of Green Ginger and pausing again, perhaps, for a stirrup-cup in the seventeenth-century Ye Olde White Harte Inn, where they took the momentous decision to defy King Charles. The panelling of its upper rooms is old and fine; I shall tell you how I used to linger there, despising my puerile glass of lemonade, while my father chatted inside the forbidden smoke room with merchants and sea-captains. These latter are indeed the very muscles of our body politic; rough, heroic men in war and peace, but in those days rather aimless when ashore and likely as not flushed and vociferous as they stood drinking in their hard bowlers and heavy overcoats. A few yards away, I insist on traversing the shopping arcade, if only to mourn the passing of those successive delights of my youth, the so-called Penny Bazaar and, at the tunnel's gloomiest point, the Ecclesiastical Repository.[6] Nearby too stands the cavernous fruit market, full of brazen-lunged salesmen and gorgeous wreaths – some of our locals are great adorners of graves, builders of monuments and frequenters of cemeteries, wherein they display a truly pathetic assiduity and extravagance.

Then suddenly we emerge, not indeed into the light, but into the shadow of what I always maintain, despite pedantic mathematical disproofs, to be infinitely the hugest parish church in England. Holy Trinity is a box-like and mainly Perpendicular building, light in construction, thanks to a marshy subsoil, slender-shafted and wide-windowed. In its chancel and transepts may be observed a fourteenth-century essay in brickwork unequalled in English architecture. One knows many a church more splendid in detail or embodying higher structural and aesthetic conceptions, yet scarcely one more fully expressive of its peculiar place and social setting. As befits the monument of Hull's earliest centuries of prosperity, it contains several tombs and as the slabs commemorating past merchant princes, notably one

in the south chancel aisle somewhat uncertainly ascribed to Sir William De la Pole. This remarkable man we may take as the symbol of an age of social transition every whit as portentous as our own, for he was the first merchant capitalist to found a great English noble family. Though probably of local origin, he moved early in life to Hull and built up a vast fortune in the wine and wool trades. By the 1330's the De la Poles were financing the ambitious Continental schemes of Edward III, who appears to have developed a genuine personal esteem for his *Mercator Regis*. This latter responded with great sacrifices on behalf of an ever-impecunious master, while at the same time using his credit at Court to secure numerous privileges for his town. Here in this windowed recess he lies sculptured in alabaster beside the figure of his wife, Catherine Norwich. He wears the long gown of a merchant, has a book in his hands and a measuring stick at his side. Inevitably one tries to trace in those austere lineaments the personality of a man who stood among the most respected and public-spirited of an age when the new capitalist was being summoned to bolster up a world of decadent and meretricious chivalry. For a moment the imaginative eye endows the face with life and then . . . back it has gone into the crude, unbreathing stone. William De la Pole's descendants became the Earls of Suffolk and were gradually uprooted from their Hull background. His son, Michael, the ill-fated favourite of Richard II, founded the Hull Charterhouse – one of the three houses in Yorkshire of that proud Carthusian Order 'never reformed because never deformed'. Its site lay some distance to the north of the town wall and is now occupied by an almshouse, the best part of which, the Georgian master's house, recently fell victim to a bomb.[7] Beneath the west end of Holy Trinity church rages a street market, raffish and gypsy-like, much as for centuries past. In youth it was pure delight to stray there, watching Jewish vendors sell their wares by Dutch auction, pestering one's elders for a tortoise or a parrot, bargain hunting amid the bookstalls, buying a vulgar packet of fried potatoes and pronouncing them twice as delicious when illicitly eaten in the open air. Facing Holy Trinity stands the brick facade of the grammar school which Bishop Alcock refounded the year after the first Tudor came to the throne, the school where our greatest citizen, Andrew Marvell, is thought to have been educated.[8] A more living interest attaches to the nearby headquarters of the Hull Trinity House, with its chapel, its perfect Georgian rooms, its portraits of admirals and relics of Captain Cook, its council chamber strewn with rushes, its pictures and models of old ships, numerous and delightful as those in the House of the Shipmen's Company at Lübeck. I doubt whether one in five hundred of Hull's population has been privileged to view the interior; it is reserved by this ancient and exclusive Corporation for the truly appreciative and the especially introduced.[9]

From the Market Place we might stroll into Lowgate, noting St. Mary's – the 'Low Church', greatly reduced by the collapse of the tower in the days of Henry VIII – and thence by Chapel Lane enter the High Street, which runs north and south along the back of the River Hull. Poorly conserved, this once famous thoroughfare now consists in the main of Victorian warehouses jostling uncomfortably together or breaking apart where some bomb fell or where some narrow staithe leads to the river quays.[10] This tributary of the Humber formed our sole medieval harbour and here barges of much the same tonnage as a sea-going vessel of De la Pole's day are still unloaded by tackle which would have presented no problems to his younger contemporary – the rascally and accomplished Shipman whom Chaucer described as without equal from 'Hulle to Cartage'. In the sadly decayed High Street, where generations of famous merchant families lived cheek by jowl with their ships, there stands yet one splendid red-brick mansion of the Elizabethan age. This we call

High Street, Hull.
(JDL)

Wilberforce House, though it could already boast a long history when the Emancipator first saw light here in 1759. It was built by the Elizabethan merchant and mayor of Hull, John Lister, whose family held the place until a few years before its purchase by the grandfather of William Wilberforce.[11]

Connoisseurs will admire the admirably restored Tudor and Georgian rooms; the simpler-minded,

Wilberforce House with the statue of William Wilberforce.
(JDL)

those fearsome and fascinating relics of slavery – spiked iron collars, rhinoceros-hide whips, placards offering rewards for runaways and the like. My children show an unaccountable fascination for the wax model of Wilberforce seated in a reconstruction of his study. More sophisticated observers will prefer the famous Van der Heist portrait of Marvell, subtle-featured as one could wish in so consummate a poet, yet withal honest and sensible as befits the incorruptible M.P. who regaled his Hull constituents with such conscientious and regular reports from London.

Standing before this portrait, you may feel it strange that a materialistic port should have brought forth, honoured and sent to Parliament two men so fine-fibred, so contemptuous of gain as were Marvell and Wilberforce. And despite them, despite many another shining exception, we remain in some important respects an uninspired community. I called Hull a boy's paradise and certainly it has never wholly satisfied the many adult spirits I have encountered there. Yet the mere charge of commercialism seems both superficial and inaccurate: Hamburg was a highly commercial city, yet its life, both before the war and amid the hideous ruins of 1945, one could not but recognise as eminently more cultured than that of Hull. It knew how to avoid *petit bourgeois* concepts, how to make commerce create a stately urban environment. Even amid political barbarism. And with Helsingfors, a port of about our own size and much more newly established, a multitude of unflattering comparisons would occur to the dullest traveller. What then are the specific qualities of this solitary large urban society of the East Riding ?

Forever despised be crude generalisations, yet there does exist something like a 'Hull mind', an outlook quite distinct from those of the rural East or the industrial West Riding.   Friendly, homely, full of grit, hospitable, our typical citizen is undoubtedly also intelligent and quick-witted; he has absorbed the stimulating atmosphere of the quayside rather than

The former Stepney Station, Beverley Road, Hull.
(JDL)

Paragon Station, Hull: the booking hall, 1903-4.
(JDL)

the deadening efficiency of the production-belt. My own conviction to this effect was strengthened by a five-months spell of testing and training Army recruits from all parts of Yorkshire. By and large I would claim that the Hull dock worker runs, intellectually speaking, several lengths ahead of the Sheffield foundryman. Yet this quick-wittedness is all too often limited by a certain insularity, a narrowness of cultural influences ascribable in part to geographical isolation. Hull forms, it is true, the central link of the economic chain between our industrial North and the Rotterdam-Hamburg-Baltic world, yet the vast majority of its citizens can claim little or no first-hand knowledge of either. Though the Humber ports afford cheap and expeditious access to the Continent,[12] the majority even of those who can afford to travel, spend their holidays year after year at local seaside resorts. Blockaded from the East Midlands by a wide and poorly-traversed river, many of them also lack appreciation for their own East Riding. The statistics of the excellent Central Library indicate that the public addicted to books is larger than the travelling public, yet in too few homes does the capacity of the bookshelves remotely begin to rival that of the wardrobes. Certain amateur dramatic groups achieve high standards amid most unpropitious surroundings, yet the excellent 'straight' theatre has always had to fight hard for existence, while the mania for watching professional football eclipses even that of the West

Riding and Lancashire. As to that lack of the visual-artistic faculty, you may prove it any day by visiting many an upper middle class household, where you will find Monarch of the Glen, the coloured photograph of the Scottish terrier, the sugary pinks and purples of Highland or Nile views still reigning in unthreatened majesty.

Accordingly Hull was, even before the war, not merely one of the more unbeauteous of our cities, but becoming rapidly uglier before one's very eyes.[13] Loathsome miles of commercial hoardings disfigured the main arteries, while the new housing estates not only removed workers miles from their work, but failed to cater for the Soul, which craves snugness, individuality, a church steeple and somewhere handy for a cup of coffee. Meanwhile, an ill-contrived scheme of slum clearance, most laudable in aim, created in the very centre of the city great arid deserts, which, after years of stagnation, still showed little sign of decreasing when the Luftwaffe came to enlarge their extent and create an even ampler paradise for the bill-sticker. At the end of the war an Abercrombie Plan, absurdly beyond economic realities, merely served to prolong the interval of paralysis. At the time I write, ten years after the serious bombing, a scattering of shops and public buildings has finally begun to fall on the desert. At least one of them, it must be conceded, deserves commendation as an example of the new British architecture which has broken away from the dull, anonymous brick box. This is the large new department store opposite the Station, light, elegant and not a little reminiscent of the Festival of Britain. In all fairness, however, this long post-war delay cannot wholly be ascribed to local divisions and muddleheaded sociology. The more aspiring citizens show a pardonable bitterness in discussing the low priorities accorded to a community which has suffered so cruelly in the common cause. They feel forgotten by a sentimental yet short-memoried nation, from which, in any event, their trials were concealed throughout the years of war by stupidly secretive official references to raids upon 'a north-eastern port'. Hull has nearly a third of a million inhabitants and is still the third port of the kingdom; it has suffered more damage than Coventry itself, yet nevertheless the geographical situation makes its claims conveniently easy to overlook, both for the nation at large and for the central planner in particular. Not for us the warm surge of feeling which, so rightly, went to the aid of poor little Lynmouth. However we may apportion the blame, some radical

rehabilitation of the central districts has long been a crying psychological need. And this area is too big to fill with shops and offices. Would that more of the people could be converted to flat-life in the manner of Social-Democrat Vienna. Certainly no number of prefabricated houses on the perimeter can atone for the spiritual depression of these

The Guildhall, Hull.
(JDL)

British twentieth century. If our response to the challenge proves at best mediocre, the reasons will lie not only in national finance and economics, not merely in our inability to afford an Abercrombie-revolution, not even with the type of sociologist who would allow no public building until every man has a 'prefab'. Our mediocrity is more likely to spring from the timid, *démodé* conventionality of our tastes in architecture, from the over-influence of people who have neither heard of Le Corbusier nor Stockholm and Aarhus, but who remain satisfied with the neo-Georgian brick rectangles so beloved of our lazier and duller architects. So let the businessman and the municipal committees realise more clearly that we are now past the middle of the twentieth century, a century which has evolved architectural idioms of extraordinary service and beauty and sincerity. The business of the patron is to select an architect with ideas and then back him with enthusiasm; the patron needs liveliness and flair, not technique or learning – after all, he need only visit Oxford to witness the recent feeble exploits of learned patrons overburdened (as we in Hull are not) by the

areas of concentrated destruction. The influence of buildings in the grand manner is more than a stimulus to business, more even than the basis of civic pride. It shapes the most intricate contours of our minds with its inescapable recall to the values of our civilisation, which, for good or ill, is still firmly based on the *civitas.* Spiritually as physically, public buildings should form the visible crown of the city; they symbolise the high aspirations which grow from and yet ennoble its economic life. Florence and Venice did not grow as museums; they were the two most prosperous trading cities of the great age of Italy. Why do their modern counterparts so seldom produce memorials of their better selves, to inspire and enrich posterity? The question carries us far beyond our present subject, yet Hull provides one of those supreme test-cases on which posterity will judge the proximity of the past. As for the architect, he must also be a good diplomat; it is his business to prevent democratic committees from erecting symbols of their own Lowest Common Denominators.

Few citizens of Hull would like their visitors to judge the physical appearance of their city, for they can certainly boast a better record in other spheres. The *élite* of brave spirits who move relatively unscathed amid the ubiquitous hoardings is larger than the casual observer would ever suppose. Of late years its confidence and its organisation have been greatly strengthened by the wide-spread stimulus exerted by the University, founded in 1927 as a University College by the great Hull philanthropist, T. R. Ferens, and made independent by Royal Charter in 1954. Rightly drawing the majority of its students from other parts of England, it nevertheless provides its region with very extensive and increasingly welcomed cultural opportunities. Chamber music, art, archaeology, history, current affairs and all the customary activities which have to pass under the unduly grim title of Adult Education now revolve in large measure around this centre.[14] Indeed, if educational institutions can produce culture, Hull should rival most English provincial cities in that somewhat amorphous commodity. It has a Training College for Teachers, a Technical College, a College of Art and Crafts[15] and numerous secondary schools, all admirable in their various functions. Indeed, I must here ask leave to acknowledge a profound debt of gratitude to one of these last, and consequently to its founder, Dr. John Hymers, who happened to be a financial genius and to retire to the local rectory of Brandesburton after a brilliant career as mathematician and President of St. John's, Cambridge. The school itself deserves a visit if one is long in Hull; it is admirably situated in grounds which were in Victorian times the Botanic Gardens. Its architect was Dr. John Bilson, a leading local practitioner of the last generation, who enjoyed international repute, especially among French scholars, as an authority upon Gothic architecture.[16]

Like so many other English provincial cities, Hull has an old-established musical tradition with a Philharmonic Orchestra, an annual Music Festival, a very fair sequence of popular classical concerts, the last especially since the birth of the Yorkshire Philharmonic.[17] It partakes fully in the great choral traditions of Yorkshire, which are gradually contriving to abandon Stainer in favour of Bach and Handel. Where sheer singing is concerned, Yorkshiremen exceed the Welsh in fullness of tone and all others in technique and emotional qualities – or so we may claim without appearing too grossly ridiculous! Talking of emotion, East Yorkshiremen, as befits a people predominantly Danish by race, are not at all dour or reluctant to show emotion, a fact clear enough from their nonconformist religious traditions. What intensity of zeal and emotion did our Victorians and Edwardians achieve! These immense Hull chapels, Bethesda, Ebenezer and the rest, built in flaming multi-coloured brick after designs prepared, one would guess, by the prophet Ezekiel after a hectic weekend in Nineveh! Those violently emotional testifyings and prayer-classes, those open-air camp-meetings where, in exuberant Old Testament phraseology, the local prophets alternately called to public repentance and denounced strong drink from the eminence of a waggonette! My own maternal grandfather was a Primitive Methodist local preacher and, of course, a Liberal in politics. Well I remember going hand-in-hand to chapel with the old man, resplendent in silk hat, morning coat, gold Albert and side-whiskers, all doubtless unmodified since 1880. Never could I seriously ridicule the idiom of his religion, for his personal life, like that of several of his associates, bore most of the marks of sanctity. In Hull, as elsewhere, it has now become too common to recall the hypocrites who accompanied the saints. A generation which boasts neither can surely cast no stone, for in England hypocrisy is not merely the homage paid by vice to virtue, it is purchase-price paid by society for sanctity. Uprooted young people without memories may easily overestimate the puritan severity of these Victorian nonconformists, who played so vast a part in shaping our northern minds and environments. At least I must record that my grandparents' strict sabbatarianism, teetotalism and fundamentalism – they had both read the whole Bible many times and 'believed its every word' – did not exclude utmost tenderness to a child, even the gift of a packet of sweets every Sunday morning, in order to brighten endless deserts of sermonising.

By comparison, how lacking in richness of persona are we, the modern bourgeoisie and tradesmen and manual workers of these northern cities, how discontented and self-centred, how incapable now of

transcending our harsh material environment, of seeing ourselves in the twin mirrors of time and eternity! Yet it would be mistaken to suppose that the volcano of northern nonconformity lies utterly extinct, though admittedly its lava-streams have ebbed and cooled. Even in those places where they have set hard and lifeless, one may find but lightly buried a variety of old relics. The modern East Riding secularist not infrequently retains a post-non-conformist mind, unliberated from many ghosts and taboos and narrownesses. All this makes a really monstrous digression as I keep you standing here in Wilberforce House before the portrait of Marvell, yet I am only half repentant; Hull is essentially a place which may only be understood by observers who look behind bricks and mortar into the spiritual history of the people.

From Wilberforce House we may reach the Humber waterfront by following the High Street southward, and nowadays with relatively little risk of being trampled to death by horse-drays or crushed by sacks of meal swaying from

Pearson Park: the cast-iron entrance arch.
(JDL)

hygienic but more magical days it had a section for live fowls, puppies, rabbits and guinea-pigs), the waterfront taverns where salts and their money are soon parted. Had we walked this way fifteen years ago, I should have pointed out gaps and repairs caused by the Zeppelin raids of my infancy, whence the most splendid memory is that of a skyborne golden cigar surrounded by beams and bursting shells. But amid the more recent havoc the gallant and long-suffering denizens no doubt sighed for the primitive warfare of 1917.[19]

the high warehouse pulleys. As a pleasanter alternative we may return to Lowgate and admire upon our walk Scheemaker's gilded statue of William III in the costume of a Roman Emperor and – a thing which would have shaken the Dutchman both mentally and physically – riding without stirrups. 'Every day, the moment King Billy hears the clock strike one,' they told me years ago, 'he dismounts and goes into the old Cross Keys[18] for dinner.' And then these heavy humorists waited for a supposedly intelligent boy to see the catch in the story.

All this neighbourhood has its own local colour compounded of a dozen typical sights – the onion-scented showrooms of the wholesale fruit merchants, the emporia of ships' husbands, who sell anything from a coil of rope to the cabin furniture of a merchantman, the iron-girdered meat market (in less

Now we quickly emerge from the dingy buildings into the blast of free air and sunlight, where the eye gains sudden freedom to leap across two miles of Humber to the Lincolnshire coast. Any fine summer morning or evening you will relish the scene from the high platform of this Victoria Pier, whence the capacious paddle-steamers voyage diagonally to New Holland.[20] Who could fail to enjoy the infinite, sun-chequered, molten turmoil of waters within the noble curve of this inland sea, the long timber-ships and grimy tramps riding at anchor, the fussily hooting tugs with their trains of lighters, and the now almost extinct sailing barges termed 'keels'. These big flat-bottomed craft seem our archetype-vessels, for hulls of a similar shape, size and construction, hulls of unknown but probably prehistoric antiquity, have recently been excavated from the Humber mud near North Ferriby[21] not many miles upstream. But such are doubtless the new fangled craft of yesterday compared with that huge dugout ship from Brigg, the great-great-grandfather of all British ships, which we boys used to regard with fitting reverence as it hung aloft side by side with the skeleton of a whale in the great hall of the Central Museum.[22] Ship, whale and museum vanished together in the late *Götterdammerung* and the first is certainly irreplaceable. As for the whale, one may at least study in the Museum of Fisheries and Shipping[23] numerous memorials of the days when Hull led the whaling ports of England. During the first quarter of the last century, about sixty Hull whalers operated two-fifths of the national industry, after which their numbers gradually dwindled and by 1869 had reached insignificance.

From our high grandstand on the waterfront you can either actually see or easily imagine the whole line of docks stretching three or four miles in either direction, each dock somewhat resembling a household with its own family of ships and merchandise, each containing its own range of nautical personalities. The Fish Dock, well out of sight up river, is perhaps the showpiece.[24] There amid hordes of high-booted men, countless barrels and stacks of ice, the trawlers hastily unload every type of catch from the princely halibut to the plebeian catfish, denizens of all the northern seas. Hull and Grimsby, the latter slightly smaller as a fishing port, occupy between them over half the national deep-sea industry. Hull claims most of the Distant Water fishing; its skippers had reached the Faroe Islands and Iceland about 1890, the White Sea by the early years of the present century and the remote Davis Strait by 1920. The trawlers are now of pre-eminent size and modernity; many contain their own freezing, fish meal and oil extraction plants. Yet trawling will never become a comfortable occupation; a disaster involving loss of life strikes some member of the Hull fleet on an average about once a year. In the autumn of 1952 the *Norman* struck a rock off the Greenland coast and of its crew of twenty only one, a boy of nineteen, swam to safety through the icy turmoil of water.

The largest docks lie downstream. The King George Dock was opened in 1914, but is still one of the largest and best equipped on this coast. It deals with coal, general cargoes and much of the grain and flour from Canada, Australia, the United States and Russia. The Victoria Dock (1850-1852)[25] is almost exclusively devoted to the importation of pit-props and other sawn wood from the Baltic; it has a system of timber transportation by 'bogies' unique to Hull. The Alexandra Dock (1885), still perhaps of most interest to a casual visitor wishing to see a variety of big modern freighters, imports timber, general cargoes, oil seeds and nuts from West Africa, South America, India and the Far East. To me, this one also has hereditary charm, as my paternal grandfather saw it built and was for many years its chief inspector. We may incidentally take this other forbear of mine as representing the rival ideology to the Nonconformist Liberalism. He was a man of calm, non-apocalyptic good sense, an Anglican churchwarden and organist, needless to say a staunch Conservative. But little of these old tensions was apparent to me when I used to visit 'Grandpa's dock' nearly forty years ago, watching with delight the thunderous showers of Canadian grain, the great hoists loading up that good English coal which once turned the wheels of continents. These were also great days for Hull shipbuilding, days too when Hull formed the headquarters of the greatest privately-owned fleet in the world, the Wilson Line, built up by Charles Henry Wilson, first Lord Nunburnholme and the veritable William De la Pole of his generation. His business *pied-à-terre* was the Bungalow (a miniature palace opposite one of Winifred Holtby's old homes and near my own present house in Cottingham) while his brother

Arthur maintained the great mansion of Tranby Croft three miles to the south. With atavistic reverence I recently acquired a fireplace (*art nouveau*, 1897) from the Bungalow and some gilded chandeliers from Tranby Croft, which latter must literally have cast light upon the great baccarat scandal of 1890, that climax of the lush plutocracy which surrounded, and occasionally embarrassed, the Prince of Wales.

In viewing the port of Hull one returns instinctively to the memory of the merchant princes and the succulent if ill-distributed plenty of the days of free trade. Nevertheless, despite two wars which have locked North Sea and Baltic for almost a decade of this century, the trade of Hull has once again become great and flourishing. In 1945, working amid the ruins of Hamburg, and a year later, reflecting (from the deck of a Russian ship off Tallinn) upon the glum sterility of the eastern Baltic, I confess I myself doubted our own revival. Phoenix-like, the world of trade has rebuked such faint-heartedness. Though Manchester runs neck-and-neck with it, Hull is in fact once more our third port and occupies almost the same percentage of English overseas commerce as in 1938.[26] To appreciate the obstacles against which this revival has been accomplished, it must first be recalled that Hull has long been primarily a place of import from the Continent. The war struck at this function in at least four important respects. It destroyed beyond hope of speedy repair certain major installations, notably those of the Riverside Quay (just west of this Pier) which provided a rapid turn-round for all classes of vessels at any state of the tide. It set a new pattern of trade which involved a dependence upon imports from transatlantic sources and hence tended to exalt the ports of the West Coast. It induced the present national stringency, leading to artificial restrictions upon all imports. It impaired the economic, and in some cases the political, freedom of our Continental business associates, friends and ex-enemies alike. To these four general disadvantages we might well add those which fell in particular upon the fishing industry, when trawlers were converted into minesweepers and when wartime price controls (under which all grades of one variety obtained the same price) made quantity rather than quality the aim, thereby reducing the ultimate demand and taste for this food.

To-day, however, many of these burdens seem greatly reduced. The Netherlands, most of our Scandinavian and Baltic clients, even the Germans, are assuming ever greater importance to a nation short of dollars. Moreover, the old contacts with more distant markets have been revived and extended. Despite certain changes of emphasis, our trade depends upon the same twenty or so basic commodities which occupied it before the war. We are importing less timber and meat, exporting far less cotton goods. Liverpool now exceeds our once phenomenal import of oil-seed. The inward traffic in grain, dairy produce and raw wool has not, however, very greatly diminished. Contrary to popular impression, we are exporting almost the same amount of coal as in 1938, and of machinery, vehicles and metals enormously more. Humberside in general and Hull in particular remain the most important wool-exporting area of the Kingdom, accounting for over half the national total. Altogether, the purposeful activities we see and sense from the Pier reflect creditably on local grit and resource. They do more, for they display the resilience of a great ring of maritime nations. Wounded sorely by that 'mischievous animal the politician', we live and work together. Even the Baltic remains undetached from our world. The mortal tragedy has not yet happened, may never happen.

Immediately to the east of the Pier the brown waters of the Hull discharge into the Humber. In earlier times the entry was protected by a row of cannon and a huge chain across the mouth of the Hull. On its opposite bank Henry VIII built a long wall to protect the harbourage and the east flank of the town. At each end of this wall stood block-houses of prodigious

strength; in its centre a still larger one dignified by the name of the Castle. Under Elizabeth all three fortresses served a melancholy purpose, for within their foul dungeons there lay many of the more obstinate and heroic Roman Catholics who defied her penal laws. A century ago these places were levelled to make way for timber yards and we have thereby lost what might have formed the finest example in England (Berwick apart) of Tudor fortification.[27]

If we proceeded upstream along the Hull we should pass some extremely picturesque groupings of ships, tall dock-side buildings and girdered bridges. We should presently reach a scenically unattractive but large and important industrial area on the north-eastern perimeter. It contains one of the world's greatest seed-crushing and oil-extracting industries; it is also a leading centre for flour-milling and the manufacture of paints, blue, starch, paper and several other prosaic but essential commodities. And I shall be suspected of no partiality if I single out for mention the great firm of Reckitt,[28] the rise of which during the last century well deserves the use of a term somewhat

over-worked in business histories – romantic. Unlike some other local firms with names of international repute, its leaders have kept their roots and conferred immense benefactions upon the city.

Unless, however, a guest were a student of manufacturing processes, one would not strongly urge him to tour industrial Hull; it lacks the manifold attractions of the port – or so it seems to one native, who must confess that in twenty years' residence he has scarcely visited it a dozen times. Quite otherwise is the case with our estuary and dockland. Every port has a type of individuality denied to industrial areas; it is palpably linked with remote and dimly imagined things. Only your very Cotswold-minded aesthete or stuffy one-track ecclesiologist would omit our river from his tour of East Yorkshire. Up here on the grandstand, we behold a living pageant of the commercial greatness of England, behold it perhaps with a certain humility. Like the Anglo-Saxons who recoiled before the mighty works of Rome at Eboracum or Verulamium, our generation might well call these *giants' works*. They are the legacy of a generation superior to our own in industry, self-sacrifice and creative enterprise.

Yet I know that, all this while, you have been admiring the immense clouds, the gilded water, the far recession of masts and cranes; you have been only half hearing my pedantries and fearing that any moment I may start quoting statistics. Whether all commerce appeals or not, the riverside is all beauty, formal, picturesque beauty, quite apart from its functions and associations. Small wonder that Hull has given birth to a long succession of marine painters.[29] For us all there are hours when this tidal river, these ships and quays, the old clustering roofs of the town, the blue, misted Lincolnshire Wolds, hours when they inspire no mere moral platitudes but simply invest themselves with the robe of beauty.

FOOTNOTES

1   Queen Victoria Square is often called City Square by locals.
2   The Dock Offices became the Town Docks Museum in 1975 and have since been renamed the Maritime Museum.
3   The Ferens Art Gallery was considerably extended in 1990. Since 1954 its collection has been discriminatingly developed and is now one of national importance.
4   In addition to the conversion of Queen's Dock into Queens Gardens, the other Town Docks are no longer in commercial use. Princes Dock is largely occupied by the shopping complex, Princes Quay, and Humber Dock and Railway Dock have become a Marina. The College of Technology, now Hull College, designed by Sir Frederick Gibberd, was built 1960-2. The projected museum referred to by Dickens was not built but the City's museums in High Street have undergone major improvements.
5   The Beverley Gate was excavated in 1988 and an amphitheatre constructed to display its history.
6   Hepworth's Arcade (1894) has been restored in 2002.
7   The master's house at the Charterhouse was reconstructed 1954-6 and the whole complex including the Georgian Chapel is in excellent condition, long recovered from its wartime damage.
8   The 'open market' west of Holy Trinity church has now been – controversially – closed and the area re-designed and re-designated as Trinity Market. For the various change of location undergone by the statue of Andrew Marvell see Gareth Watkins,

Andrew Marvell and his wandering statue (Hull City Museums, Art Gallery Archives, 1996).
9   Group visits to Trinity House can be made by special arrangements.
10 Great interest has developed over the past half-century in restoring Hull's High Street and, designated as a Conservation Area and with great attention paid to its historic buildings and its ambience, it is one of the City's most visited attractions.
11 Many improvements have been made to Wilberforce House (No. 25), with fine displays in the adjacent Georgian Houses and subsidiary buildings. The dating of Wilberforce House (No. 25) to the Elizabethan period is now questioned: stylistically the façade is c.1660. Other great merchant houses in High Street have become more prominent since Dickens wrote. The Georgian Maister House (No. 160), then Victorianised and serving as offices, was later sensitively restored and transferred to the National Trust, its only property in the area. Blaydes House (No. 6), also Victorianised, was acquired by the Georgian Society for East Yorkshire and has now been sold to the University of Hull for its Maritime Historical Studies Centre. The facade of Crowle House (No. 46) has also been restored.
12 Since Dickens wrote thousands of local people have become familiar with Europe, particularly with the Netherlands and Belgium, through the excellent service provided by North Sea Ferries.
13 The criticism of Hull in the immediate pre-war period is a subjective opinion which facts do not entirely support. Hull was a smart shopping centre with a lively social life. Although the building of Ferensway (1931), which removed much substantial housing, did not result in commercial development on the scale anticipated, Hull was progressing well with the clearance of slum property and the building of new residential areas, both public and private, until the devastation of the Blitz. The Abercrombie Plan was, fortunately, a failure as it would have meant the destruction of buildings and features now highly valued. Dickens is referring to Hammonds Store, built in a modern style to replace the one lost in the Blitz. Interestingly, he was sympathetic to this new architectural vision, though the building probably does not merit the praise he accorded it nearly 50 years ago. The standard guide to the area's buildings, Nikolaus Pevsner and David Neave, *Yorkshire: York and the East Riding* (2nd edn 1995), does, however, state that 'it has worn well'. Hull's delay in post-war rebuilding of its blitzed central areas saved it from the worst of the 1960s architecture which has blighted other cities. Local experience of tower blocks of flats has not been an outstanding success.
14 Hull University's much valued Department of Adult Education has been replaced by the Centre for Lifelong Learning.
15 Major reorganisation in 1976 amalgamated these college (including the College of Commerce and the Nautical College)

into two institutions: the Hull College of Further Education and the Hull College of Higher Education. The former is now Hull College and the latter, after a number of name changes, the University of Lincoln.

16 Hymers College, a rigidly male institution, particularly under the autocratic and misogynist W. V. Cavill, headmaster in the latter part of Dickens's period as a pupil, took its first girl into the Sixth Form in 1971 and became fully co-educational in 1989.

17 Dickens means the Yorkshire Symphony Orchestra, 1947-55.

18 The Cross Keys, headquarters of Liberal candidates in 19th-century parliamentary elections, was demolished in 1937.

19 Hull's first Zeppelin raid was on 6 June 1915. In all there were seven raids.

20 The New Holland ferry ceased on the opening of the Humber Bridge, 1981.

21 The first two Ferriby boats were excavated in 1946.

22 The museum in Albion Street was demolished in an air raid in 1943.

23 Contents of the Museum of Fisheries and Shipping in Pickering Park have been transferred to the Maritime Museum, Queen Victoria Square.

24 St. Andrew's Dock, the Fish Dock, was closed in 1975.

25 The Victoria Dock has been closed and the site used for the Victoria Dock Village, a major development involving public and private cooperation in the creation of a residential community. See Colin McNichol, *Hull's Victoria Dock Village* (Beverley, 2002).

26 Hull is no longer the country's third port.

27 The fortifications known as the Citadel were excavated in 1988 before work commenced on the Victoria Dock Village. A bartizan known locally as a watch tower, which became a feature of East Park, has now been returned to a spot in the Victoria Dock Village not far from its original location.

28 Reckitt's is now Reckitt Benckiser Healthcare (UK) Ltd.

29 Most notable of the maritime artists was John Ward. See Arthur Credland, *Maritime Painting in Hull Through Three Centuries* (Hull and Cherry Burton, 1993).

Bridlington, Driffield, Holderness

The notion of Holderness as a mere fenny plain between Wold and sea dates back at least to Chaucer, who makes his Summoner say:

> Lordinges, ther is in Yorkshire, as I gesse,
> A mersshy contree called Holdernesse.

The guess was in fact none too comprehensive, for once you pass beyond the winter-flooded carrs either side of the River Hull, you enter an area thickly covered with small glacial mounds and morainic ridges, which, along with copses, woods and winding streams, give the land a sinuous line quite distinct from the squarely-sliced pancake of the fens. This had been a main granary of the North centuries before Drayton made the East Riding boast,

> Rich Holderness I have, excelling for her grain.

These cornlands, assisted by the prosperity of the old Humber ports, afforded an economic background to the splendid outburst of building between the thirteenth and fifteenth centuries, the episode which has alone put our remote coastal plain on the cultural map of Europe by leaving several glorious churches, two of them unexcelled of their types throughout Christendom. Since then, drainage and reclamation have greatly extended and diversified the pattern of agriculture. The soil itself ranges between three types of clay, besides gravel patches, riverside warp and peaty carrs, with the result that no general rotation of crops can obtain. Wheat, barley, turnips, oats, beans, clover, mustard and fine permanent grass combine to variegate the miniature landscapes gained from knoll and tower.

As befits a coastal plain forever torn by the sea and built up by the river, Holderness is full of strange aquatic phenomena. First among these – at least if, rather un-historically, we include the Bridlington area in our subject – come the 'gypseys' or intermittent streams which run from the chalklands to the sea after rainy seasons, or, as the ancient superstition has it, to portend battle, murder and sudden death. They are mentioned not only by Camden and Drayton, who call them 'vipseys', but by that twelfth-century native of Bridlington, William of Newburgh: *famosae illae aquae quas vulgo Gipse vocant.* The chief of these harbingers of disaster flows, when it decides to flow, down the Gypsey Race to the sea at Bridlington; needless to say, so many centuries of experience have enabled it to gauge the international situation very astutely and it flowed with due vigour in 1914 and 1939, fertilising luxuriant crops of letters in the newspapers.

Less sinister are the Naffers of Nafferton, not the county family one might at first sight presume, but something even more bucolic: a series of clear springs which gush out from the chalk at several places in or near that locally proverbial township and especially at one end of the big village pond,

Again, Holderness has in Hornsea Mere the largest lake in Yorkshire, a limpid mirror two miles long, its banks reedy and wooded, its islets with their heronries and rare wildfowl – the Great Crested Grebe, the Pochard, the Bittern – in delightful variety and profusion. So rich was its fishing in those ages when fresh water fish commanded respect that the abbots of Meaux and St. Mary's fought out their rival claims by a battle of hired champions, presumably experienced professionals, since the contest lasted all day without fatal results.

Both Holderness and the eastern Wolds admit a record of terrible storms, one of which in 1732 paralysed the parish clerk of Hornsea just when he was engaged in storing smuggled goods inside the church. Another in 1839 killed the whole family of the miller of Nafferton, against whom history records no such reproach, while one July Sunday in 1892 a waterspout almost devastated the village of Langtoft,

leaving to this day cruel scars down the Wold. As for other dire climatic auguries, I have myself twice seen a mirage of the Hull skyline – chimneys, cranes and all – from the coast very near Bridlington and, though on the second occasion I was soon afterwards grossly overcharged for a brandy and soda in a seafront saloon, I cannot claim that these phenomena were accompanied by any really adequate reward for my sins.

To leave the dramatic chalk-cliffs, the menacing swell, the northern gales of Flamborough Head, for the normal calm of Bridlington Bay and the soft brown coast of Holderness is to enter another world. 'In short,' writes Blackmore, 'to have rounded that headland from the north is as good as to turn the corner of a garden wall in March, and pass from a buffeted back, and bare shivers, to a sunny front of hope all as busy as a bee, with pears spurring forward into dreamy buds of promise, peach trees already in a flush of tasselled pink, and the green lobe of the apricot shedding the snowy bloom.' Such orchard-like calm is scarcely characteristic of Bridlington's promenade, a place where the variety-fearing population of Hull, having contemplated itself in its own streets for fifty weeks of the year, re-assembles to continue the process in other surroundings for the remaining fortnight. That this is a cheerful, well-conducted watering-place with a colourful harbour and good facilities for yachting, fishing and dancing, I do not deny, yet I am no adequate publicity agent, for personally I prefer my resorts vaster, more vulgar and opulent, with huge Kursaals and casinos built on replicas of the Hanging Gardens of Babylon, colonnaded emporia and gilded hotels, their dining rooms elevated like pagodas, gigantic dance-palaces made of coloured glass, full of foreign gigolos, sun-tanned goddesses, orchid-scent and negroid rhythms, in short, resorts worthy of the combined pens of Gautier and Aldous Huxley. Even in Yorkshire, why be content with less?

As for the old harbour of Bridlington, it had – quite

13. *Trinity House, Hull (left)* (JDL)

14. *Hull's Garden Village* (JDL)

apart from some recent bombing – a dramatic moment in 1643, when Queen Henrietta Maria landed here from the Continent with arms for her hard-pressed husband, Charles I. Four pursuing Roundhead ships put in close to her house on the Quay and, as she wrote to Charles, 'before I could get out of bed, the balls came whistling upon me in such shape that you may easily believe I loved not such music'. Having left the house to gain the shelter of a ditch, she remembered her ugly lapdog, Mitte, and insisted with typical gallant obstinacy on returning for it, though the bombardment continued heavy and a sergeant was killed but a few paces distant. A more accurate aim would, incidentally, still have saved the Stuarts much trouble, since with all her Bourbon talent for learning and forgetting nothing, she survived as their consistently evil genius well the into the reign of her son.

The resort should properly be called Bridlington Quay, since the old and original Bridlington is a little, unvisited market town over a mile inland. Its houses cluster round the Priory, that still impressive torso of an old religious house which played no slight role in earlier centuries of Yorkshire history. The present fabric consists of a nave – always used, even in monastic days, for parish worship – and two very dissimilar towers. It lacks choir and transepts; its south wall, which once adjoined the Prior's lodging, remains for this reason partially 'blind'; the arcading of the interior has also been imperfectly developed on that side. Yet, despite such shortcomings, Bridlington Priory preserves a dignity far surpassing that of many more fortunate churches. Offhand, I can think of four features especially demanding notice: the splendidly ornate south-western tower; the north porch, even though its upper story betrays the restorer's hand; the unsurpassed west doorway – so much finer than any at York – with its leafy hood and finial, its foliated capitals, its mouldings laden with vines and acorns; the whole south side of the nave with its huge triforium, one of the grandest single conceptions of our fourteenth-century northern architects.

The last Prior of Bridlington, William Wood, dangled at Tyburn for his share in the Pilgrimage of Grace, and a year later Henry VIII's commissioners, according to their own accounts extant in the State Papers, set about demolishing the Priory with such needless savagery that we may consider ourselves fortunate to possess even this much of a church which almost rivalled Beverley in the days of its glory. Nearby stands the Bayle Gate,[1] constructed by the canons about 1390; before being recently pensioned off as a museum and as the meeting place of the local historical society, it was in service successively as the Prior's courtroom, a prison for sailors under the Commonwealth, a nonconformist conventicle under Charles II, a barracks during the Napoleon-scare and since then as a school. Nor must you leave the precincts without observing that iron collar attached by a chain to the wall under the south-west tower. This seems to have adorned the necks of slanderers, scolds and other bores, a type of psychotherapy beloved of our ancestors and – could the Church but recover its old authority and prestige – long overdue for revival in many parishes.

Of the villages near Bridlington, both Rudston and Burton Agnes present features of much interest. The churchyard of the former contains a gigantic monolith twenty-five feet in height and penetrating as far beneath the ground; a mysterious and antediluvian object regarded with fitting reverence by local opinion. In the same churchyard, yet far more precious to us, is the grave of Winifred Holtby, that valiant, liberal-hearted crusader, whose true fame lies in no mere armful of very competent fiction and sound journalism, but in a short life strenuously devoted to humanity. Yet this land was her home; she had a faithful eye for its contours and characters; as for its social problems, she could see them through the experienced eyes of her mother, who for many years lived at Rudston, a prominent figure in East Riding public life. *South Riding* may not ultimately rank as the outstanding masterpiece hailed by certain critics, but, if asked for the most faithful 'documentary' of our province, one could recommend no other book. On the grave here in Rudston is represented an open book with the words:

> God give me work till my life shall end
> And life till my work is done.

Only a complacent observer would suppose the second prayer to have been granted, for in these years of humanitarian and cultural recession, we can ill spare Miss Holtby, who might by now have attained the height of her powers and influence.

Along the Kilham road near Rudston I remember attending during the thirties the excavation of three tessellated pavements, which turned out to be admirable examples of native provincial art during the later period of Roman occupation. So long as this artist confined his efforts to geometrical 'rug-patterns' or even dolphins and porpoises, he remained on safe ground. When, however, he tackled the subject of Venus at the Bath, or a series of hunting scenes, he administered a hearty blow to the picturesque pedants who lecture so gaily on the Classical and the Ancient World. Attended by a merman with one of those back-scratchers beloved of the best Roman society, Love's Goddess arose from the bath, still holding the apple once given her by Paris. But as to this gentleman's taste one felt signal doubts, for never was more shapeless baggage depicted by any monkish miniaturist. Let us conclude that, like the poor Romano-British mosaic worker, his patrons, the Yorkshire landowners of that age, held the Glory that was Greece in about as much esteem as an average Mid-Western meat-packer and, in fact, valued the mere anecdotal subject to the exclusion of its artistic form.[2]

Burton Agnes has a charming Elizabethan mansion, the seat of the Wickham-Boynton family, who open it to the public on certain days of the week. On its west side may be seen the remains of the Old Hall, now preserved by the Office of Works and showing a Norman undercroft, part of the house built by Roger de Stuteville about 1173. In the fourteenth century this house

Farmyard, Burton Fleming.
(JDL)

15. *The Marina, Hull* (JDL)

16. *Riverhead, Driffield*

17. *Skipsea Castle Motte* (JG)

18. *Sunk Island, looking towards Ottringham church: the great skies of Holderness*

passed to the ancestors of Sir Henry Griffith, who ultimately built the present hall during the last two years of Queen Elizabeth. Half a century later it went to the related and even more ancient family of Boynton, who migrated here from their old home at Barmston, a few miles distant upon the coast. The gate house with its four pepper-pot turrets and caryatids is unquestionably the most perfect and satisfying part of the group of buildings. The house itself has not the unspoiled unity of a really top-rank late Tudor mansion such as Montacute, since the original windows of its entrance front were replaced by Georgian windows – this not long before the destruction of a beautiful long gallery with a waggon-vaulted ceiling[3]. The authentic aspect of the house may best be appreciated on the north and west fronts, little altered since their construction. The Great Hall has two spectacular, even sensational features: the great stone and alabaster chimney-piece with its relief of the Wise and Foolish Virgins and the oak and plaster screen on the west wall representing the Evangelists. the Sybils and the Twelve Tribes. The former of these reputedly came from Barmston; it accordingly shows the arms of Sir Thomas Boynton (1544-1587), his third wife, Frances Frobisher (a cousin of the Doncaster seaman), and his fourth wife, Alice Tempest.

The furnishings and pictures in these and the several other rooms shown are of variable importance, but include some fine items: there are two Gainsborough landscapes and some good family portraits, one by Reynolds and another by that interesting painter Philippe Mercier, who settled in York during the middle years of the eighteenth century and received innumerable commissions from the prosperous Yorkshire gentry. The outstanding feature of the Drawing Room is the oak mantelpiece representing the *Dance of Death*, a superb *tour de force* by a craftsman who should prove identifiable since he must have ranked among the greatest in Europe during the earliest years of the seventeenth century.

The present owner of Burton Agnes has formed an attractive collection of modern French and English paintings; it includes some moderate examples, of Renoir, Pissaro, Bonnard, Vuillard, Utrillo, Sickert, John and Duncan Grant. After the Ferens Gallery in Hull, which happens to have few French items, this collection may fairly claim local importance in the Riding, an area not conspicuously provided with specimens of recent and contemporary painting.[4]

The architectural flair of Sir Henry Griffith was not shared by the assigns of his son, whose heavy and hideous tomb with its skulls, bones and slate coffins, spreads depression from the so-called 'Griffith Dormitory' in the north aisle of the church. Near it a splendid tomb commemorates an ancestor, Sir Walter Griffith (c.1481): in place of the kneeling 'weepers' of a late period, Sir Walter's son and daughter are here quaintly represented by miniature recumbent figures alongside their life-sized parents, he as a little knight, she in the latest fashions of the day, but neither of them much above eighteen inches long. The church itself has a good transitional arcade, but was otherwise 'restored' and churchwardenised in 1840 by Archdeacon Wilberforce, son of the liberator. The churchyard path is covered by an ancient tunnel of clipped yews, as solid and gloomy as the entrance to an underground station. Burton Agnes should be visited on a bright summer day. Though admittedly among the most beautiful places in the Riding, it seems on a leaden afternoon a trifle overweighted by the shadows of the past. In such places I cannot help seeing out of the corner of my eye the shades of that heavy-booted generation of squires who snatched power and wealth from the palsied hands of the Church, and then, having duly qualified for a place in Spelman's *History and Fate of Sacrilege,* proceeded to expiate their offences by clanking chains, exuding sensations of icy cold and smells of musty cerements, even carrying their bearded heads under their arms about the draughty passages. With these essentially unromantic companions we are less troubled in East

Lund village green, with cross and All Saints church, left background).
(JDL)

Atwick village green with shaft of cross, possibly 15th-century.
(JDL)

19.   *Beverley Beck*

20.   *North Bar Without, Beverley*

21. *St. Mary's church, Beverley: Victorian flying buttresses on the medieval south transept*

22. *Beverley's Georgian Market Cross, Saturday Market*

Yorkshire than elsewhere, perhaps because we possess only two or three Tudor manor houses with the proper background. Which from a writer's viewpoint is a pity, and would tempt me, where my honesty less rigid, to transfer to some local setting the anecdote of my meeting with that avaricious Elizabethan ghost Buttoncap in the east wing of an ancient Northamptonshire rectory, and how he stood a full five minutes by the bed of the sergeant major, whom I, full of experimental zeal, had ordered to sleep in the ghost room . . . For all that, the East Riding abounds in more *recherché* visitants. Here at Burton Agnes Hall, a whole team of poltergeists played havoc at least as lately as 1850, and more especially whenever a certain skull, reputedly that of a builder of the house, was removed. An oddly similar tradition used to attach to the manor of Lund, where the owners finally had to humour the ghosts by walling up the skull in an attic. Between Skipsea and Atwick a headless rider terrified late-returning revellers, though less aggressively than the headless woman, who, at White Cross between Leven and Ruston, would occasionally leap up behind a horseman and slap his ears. The willow-hung pool between Atwick and Bewholme was the haunt of the Halliwell Boggle, while a similar hobgoblin used to infest Brigham Lane end. On the hill forming the eastern slope of Nafferton Slack a great stone glowed at night, forming the portal of a hall frequented by troops of gaily dressed elves, and from inside the great tumulus, Willy How, near Wold Newton, might be heard the sound of midnight revelry. Such stories continued to receive sober credence fifty or sixty years ago, while earlier in the nineteenth century witches maintained their practices at Bridlington and Weaverthorpe, the latter boasting a certain old Nancy Rowley, who, on the night she died, 'flew ower Driffield chotch on a blazin' besom'.

Great Driffield is a little town in the same idiom as Market Weighton and Pocklington, situated in a pleasant park-like countryside where a number of trout streams join to form the River Hull. Speaking of trout streams, it seems worthy of remark that the Driffield Anglers' Club has enjoyed a fame based upon no mere hearsay, for trout of five pounds have been very commonly caught, while one monster, taken in 1832 and publicly exhibited for many years, measured 32 inches in length, 21 in circumference and weighed 17 pounds.

Though none too familiar with contemporary life in Driffield, I cannot help sharing the suspicion of a certain old native who thinks the town is not quite what it was.[5] In a topographical account published just a century ago, I read that Driffield then had a Corn Exchange, four banks, a farmers' club, a mechanics' institute, a gaol, several foundries, two boarding schools for young gentlemen and several important private residences. Nor are my predecessor's claims thereby exhausted, for he tells also of Mr. Coates's bull *Patriot*, which about 1820 had fetched 500 guineas, and of the superlative breeding of Leicester sheep: 'there is perhaps no part of the world in which they arrive at greater perfection'. Another notice of a type which, judging by its frequency, engaged the passionate concern of our great-grandfathers, consists of the fact that Great Driffield was a Discharged Vicarage, while Little Driffield was a mere Perpetual Curacy. We are then bidden to note that 'the air is pure and salubrious', a feature made all the more remarkable in that 'the manufacture of *Artificial Manure* is carried on here to a considerable extent'. But the beauty of these italics, so beloved of the time, shines out to the ultimate advantage in the staccato but golden period: 'There are several good *Breweries.*' A profane scientist, to whom I showed this account, now discerns the heart of the distinction between Great Driffield and its puny neighbour; he stubbornly rejects the view that its greatness lay in mere ecclesiastical and statistical primacy, but would derive it rather from this acknowledged pre-eminence in the art of fermentation, which has, he correctly observes, now become the subject of a professorial chair at one of our noble universities.

Driffield's most distinguished inhabitant was a man little regarded by his local contemporaries or, indeed, by their successors. The name of Benjamin Fawcett the colour-printer may be ranked without impropriety alongside that of Baxter himself. Born at Bridlington in 1808, he began his career in Driffield by producing copybooks at unprecedentedly low prices. About the middle of the century he gave up the retail trade and settled at East Lodge, where he perfected a new and original process of fine printing in colours. Amongst the best known of his productions are the six volumes of Morris's *British Birds* and the five of Bree's *Birds of Europe*. The book, *Beautiful Leaved Plants*,[6] was selected by the executive of the Paris Exhibition for presentation to the Empress Eugénie and, as befitted his international reputation, the printer received letters of congratulation from Queen Victoria and the Prince Consort. Like many other brilliant technologists, Fawcett was not outstandingly successful as a businessman, though others profited extensively from his discoveries. His immense *County Seats of Great Britain* contained 240 coloured plates and some 2,400 engraved blocks; it is said to have cost him almost the whole of the £30,000 which he received from the publishers, while these latter netted at least £100,000. Fawcett is described as unassuming and retiring, but extremely courteous; certainly he was little known in Driffield, whence throughout so many decades he issued a whole library of exquisite books. If he did not invite confidences, his fellow-townsmen were doubtless in their turn a little incurious about such luxuries as books. And to this day, so certain educationalists tell me, Driffield cannot without risk of exaggeration be described as the Athens of the North.

For all that, the neighbouring village of Emswell produced the most valuable farming book of the seventeenth century, one without which writers on the agricultural science of that age would be left standing at the post. Its author was the squire Henry Best, who in 1618 purchased the estate from an elder brother and subsequently worked it until his death in 1645. He was a hard-headed man intent on writing a technical and detailed manual; it approaches its subject without Shakespearian folklore and hobgoblins, with none of the Theocritan romanticism of an Isaac Walton. Even though on one occasion Best inserts a page 'concerninge our Fashions att our country weddinges' (between mowing instructions and 'observations concerninge Beastes'), he is mainly interested in the business negotiations which then gave a French flavour to matrimony. He has also some first-rate information concerning all the fairs of the East Riding, once so numerous. For the rest he will give you a thousand tips and wrinkles – how to choose a good ram, to make a ewe suckle another's lamb, to thatch a house, to hire a farm-servant, to eradicate robber-bees, to make earthern floors, to keep 'waines from wette', even how by the custom of the country you divide up a family of cygnets whose parents belong to different owners and who are hatched on the land of a third person. The book is essentially an agricultural testament for family use; it treats all these matters with the precise local examples and proper names which redouble its value for the East Yorkshire historian; like its own style and language, it seems to grow from the good earth of the Riding; it provides the perfect corrective to the *hey nonny, nonny* version of old English rural life.

Among ecclesiologists the Driffield area seems less widely known than it deserves, particularly in view of its extraordinary content of Norman architecture. The main attraction of Great Driffield church lies, however, in a fifteenth-century tower so finely proportioned as to take a high place even in that golden age of English tower-building. Its western face shows several coats of arms, including that of Hotham, with which ancient family tradition connects its origin. According to one version, a member of the family erected it to absolve himself from a vow to go on a pilgrimage to the Holy

23.   *Newbegin Beverley: one of Beverley's fine Georgian streets*

24.   *New Walk, Beverley*

Sepulchre; following another version, he sought thereby to atone for the sin of incontinence. It would be invidious even for a hard-bitten historian of Yorkshire society to express a preference for one or other of these stories; after all, the story about broken pilgrimage vows is told of so many Yorkshire barons that it may in one or two cases be true. As for incontinence, it is so brazenly acknowledged in the early wills of northern gentry that one would suppose the founder of Driffield tower to be atoning thus expensively only through exceptional piety, or as a result of incontinence so widespread as to expose him to the direst penalties of the ecclesiastical courts.

Driffield church has also an interesting Transitional nave with round-headed arcades and clerestory windows; the font is also of this same late twelfth century. Several neighbouring churches show work of earlier date. That of Little Driffield is basically Norman, as indicated by the chancel arch, which, somewhat exceptionally, should be viewed from the east side. As long before the Norman age as the period which separates us from Henry VIII, King Aldfrith of Northumbria (d.705) had been buried here in the chancel. In his case we have a more respectable choice of traditions; he was either wounded to death in a battle or struck down by divine wrath for disobeying a papal injunction. The commemoration tablet in the choir apparently replaces an ancient Latin inscription noticed by Leland. Four miles to the south-west stands the much more important church of Kirkburn, one which, among the Norman monuments of the East Riding, is often regarded as outshining Newbald itself. Its chancel arch and south doorway, each with three orders, form magnificent examples of the so-called Yorkshire Norman style of c.1150-1170, while the font is usually dated not much later than the Conquest itself. On the upper tier of the font we have probably the Baptism, the Charge to St. Peter and the Ascension. The animal motifs on the lower tier have been the subject of much contention, one expert holding that they represent the earliest of all European versions of the story of Reynard the Fox, another, more feasibly, that the animals are coming to reverence an Agnus Dei. All these features are fully described in the recent handbook to the church, perhaps the best guide of its type available in an East Yorkshire parish.[7] The chancel, barbarously 'restored' in late Georgian times, had to be completely rebuilt a century ago; the task was quite ably executed by Pearson in his somewhat hard-faced manner. The alabaster reredos, subsequently designed by Street for Sir Tatton Sykes, is excellent for its period. Somewhat to the north, Garton-on-the-Wolds has a church with important Norman elements, while Kilham and Fridaythorpe, though somewhat further afield, lie well within the compass of a short afternoon motor tour and complete as remarkable a local series of this period as may be found anywhere in England.

Passing south-eastward from Driffield, you enter the official Seignory of Holderness and begin to meet its characteristic place-names. They are hollow, sad-sounding names: Ulrome, Nunkeeling, Roos, Waxholme, Withernsea, Hollym, Paull, Boreas Hill, Sunk Island and Spurn. Repeat them over and over again like a spell and you will slowly evoke from his depths the spirit of Holderness, the spirit of crumbling shores and drowned churches, of a vast tidal estuary with endless weedy mudflats, of cities thrown up, then swallowed by the waves, of a six-mile spit of sand, a lost ship out on the wastes of water, a lone lighthouse between two oceans, where the enormous pressure of the east wind drives the massed cavalcades of thunder across the coasts. These names are charged with music and poetry, poetry one feels too deeply to dare write – at last the thoughts beside which mere word-spininng seems even more vulgar than tears. South Holderness is your true barometer of poetic sensibility: if you think it merely another ugly bit of east coast plain, say like the strip between Newcastle and Whitley Bay, you do not possess what is required; you should give up *belles lettres* for ballistics, abandon Baudelaire for Bradshaw. Ulrome,

Nunkeeling, Paull, Boreas Hill . . . need one write another word on Holderness? Is not the sad-eyed *genius loci*, his slender form swathed in blue-green mantle, already taking you by the hand?

But Holderness shows also a long and fascinating human story. At Ulrome was unearthed a primeval lake dwelling, its wooden platform sixty by ninety feet, its great piles driven deep into some mere which itself vanished centuries before history was written. To the very unclassical Romans of Rudston we have already alluded. At Roos near Withernsea was discovered the celebrated model ship made long ago by some incompetent carver, whether Viking or pre-Roman has long been argued. It has a standing crew of four, one with club and shield, others with eyes of quartz beads, all incredibly naive and almost as primitive as some of the objects evolved by petty wartime profiteers in the toy-market.

The Conqueror made Holderness a great feudal seignory, granting it to Drogo de Brevere, a Flemish adventurer alleged by the local chronicler of Meaux to have killed his wife, a relative of the King. Drogo's native business instinct seems, if anything, to have been stimulated by his sojourn among the Yorkshiremen, since, faced by this awkward predicament, he rushed to see William before the ugly news got out, and successfully extracted a substantial loan to further his own rapid exit to the Continent. The original headquarters of this Norman lordship lay at Skipsea and has left the most impressive early feudal relic in the Riding. The castle of Drogo lies to the landward side of Skipsea village: a huge *motte* or mound, in its eastern flank a fragment of a wing-wall built of sea-beach cobbles embedded in mortar. At a furlong's distance runs a crescentic earth-rampart upon an equally grand scale. In all likelihood, this bailey never encircled the *motte*, but formed a separate enclosure, protected on its unwalled side by a pond crossed by a wooden bridge. Opposite the depression in the Bail Welts, to give the ramparts their local name, one may trace the four footmarks, placed at proper fighting distance, of the duelling brothers, footmarks which an obscure folk-memory of some family quarrel has caused the villagers to perpetuate from generation to generation. Here too, not many years ago, a spectral White Lady used to throw down all new stiles and fences which obstructed her evening walk; she was identified – though doubtless only by the learned – with the unfortunate wife of Drogo. Yet archaeology and folklore apart, the whole place harmonises to perfection with the atmosphere of a spring picnic, with a pale rainy sky, its silences deepened by the startled call of a blackbird. Climbing the mound you see down below the white blossoms of the ranunculus shining like stars in the stagnant moat; the summit reveals a wide expanse of sea, the cliffs of Flamborough silvered by a tantalising shaft of sun.

During the Angevin reigns Skipsea in the hands of the Albermarles became a centre of baronial resistance to the Crown. It was besieged by the fiery Henry II and finally demolished by Hubert de Burgh, minister of the youthful Henry III. Henceforth the seignory lay at several periods in the hands of the Crown, its head being transferred to Burstwick, near the port of Hedon and amid the rich grainlands of southern Holderness. Here in 1304 we find Edward I personally issuing letters patent and, two years later, imprisoning the wife of his enemy, Robert Bruce. Again at Burstwick in 1323 stayed his poor mechanic-minded son, Edward of Carnavon, while courtiers, clerks and menials consumed the manorial stocks hoarded against their coming. No ruins of the building remain above ground, but the site should be excavated when opportunity serves.

To the great ones of the Middle Ages, the wealth of Holderness made it a key district; their leisurely movements between north and south were far from being glued, like those of modern notabilities, to the Great North Road. Thence by the revenges of time, the fall of castles and monasteries, the expansion of new grain-areas, the rise of Hull to the westward, the centralisation of road and rail travel upon York and London, Holderness tended to become something of a medieval museum inhabited by little people with small memory of its past importance, a forgotten, intensely rural area with great neglected churches, an area for the vegetation of slow-going squires and an insular peasantry, archaic in both mental interests and manner of speech.

Even, however, in this backwater, the peasant age is at last drawing to its close; no longer are mind and language to strongly moulded by local ground and circumstance. During the mere twenty-five years in which I have observed these things, the East Yorkshire dialect and mode of self-expression has been very perceptibly ironed out by radio, talking-film and externally-trained school teachers. No longer are East Yorkshire boys taught by that broad-spoken master to whom even rural parents complained that he was not teaching their offspring to speak 'fine enough'. So the pedagogue, once alone with his charges, turned on them with energy: 'Noo, lads! Sum o' yer feythers has been tellin' o' ma 'at ya deean't speeak fahin eneaff. Noo, ya mun all larn ti speeak fahin, an' if ye deean't, ah'll smash ivvry yan o' yer scaups.'

For these choicer dialect-forms one must rely increasingly upon old people, from whom, nevertheless, much quiet enjoyment may still be derived, if only the outsider will abandon any trace of patronage and recognise this language for what it is – a most ancient and authentic relic of the past, closely linked with Danish forms, steering clear of Latin roots with great ingenuity, yet full of fine, forceful terms, of *nuances* untranslatable into cold print. Moreover, the total vocabulary of the old labourer is far greater than you would guess on casual contact, for it includes a technical farming terminology which – at any rate not many years ago – used to be widely transferred in picturesque metaphor to other uses, as, for example, when an irate father, in place of the usual 'daft-heead' would call his son a 'dossel-heead',

a dossel being the straw knob on top of a stack.

This peculiar vowel 'eea' is most likely to puzzle unaccustomed listeners, for it substitutes itself in all sorts of places: 'beeats' for boots, 'eneeaf' for enough, and so on. A still more fascinating form is the mingled 't' and 'th', which needs practice to imitate successfully: 'Set-therda' being the day before Sunday. The short *u* is positively prohibited and all *u's* must be very broad and long, while the long *i* becomes 'ah', – 'mahnd' for mind.

Nor is the sound *ur* much liked, so durst becomes 'do'st' and word, 'wo'd'. And do not say to a child, 'Who's your father?', or you may get the answer, 'Vary well thank ye.' As for odd words and expressions you may find useful in conversation, 'starved' means cold; 'badly' – unwell; 'dowly' – depressed; 'tew' – knock about; 'smitting' – infectious; 'teem' – pour; 'mafted' – overcome, suffocated; 'lingy' – lean, loose-built; 'nattery' – crotchety; to 'tak' on' – get upset; 'throng' – much occupied; 'hefted' – provided with, as in 'well wi' brass', of a well-to-do acquaintance.

Such particulars constitute the merest externals of a spoken language wherein inflexion and syntax are so closely allied with the very type of mental tendencies they express – in particular a blend of canny humour with cautious understatement. 'Ah deean't mahnd if ah deea' usually signifies glad acceptance; if a man is a noted success at his job, he 'frames middlin'; if he almost certainly means to do something, he only admits, 'mebbe ah will'; if a labourer eats his head off, the farmer's wife will say, 'he's better to keep a month than a year'. Sometimes humour and caution may blend rather grimly as in the true story of the widower, who, having been bereaved no less than three times, was asked whether he intended a fourth wedding: 'Naay, nut ah; what wi marryin' on 'em an what wi' buryin' on 'em, it's ower expensive. Ah can't affo'd it na moor.'

As an example of local character and language I have compiled, with some little inspiration from Morris's *Yorkshire Folk-Talk,* the following brief bar-parlour dialogue between two middle-aged farm labourers. I have myself heard all these expressions during quite recent years, though not in this degree of concentration.

Bill: *(offers drink)* Cum thi ways in an' sit ya doon.

Tom: Ah deean't mahnd if ah deea. Ah'm ommost mafted, it's that wahm.

Bill: Ay, it *is* that *(produces a brace of rabbits from behind the bench)*. Hoo's *them* for ye ?

Tom: Mah wo'd, but them's gran' 'uns!

Bill: Ay well, an' hoo's thissen, Tom?

Tom: Ah's middlin'. Hoo's ye muther?

Bill: T' owd lass is nobbut badly. Doctther says sha's gotten 'eart disease, an' sha can't bahd ti be clashed or putten aboot, or owt; it tews her sadly. An' it's dowly wi'er on me own . . .

Tom: Ah'm suprahsed ye nivver married, Bill!

Bill: Mebbe ah will when sha's gone. Ah *was* coortin' ye knaw, but Muther wasn't sharin' wi' onnybody. Sha's lahtle, but sha's all theer. Ah cums back wun Munda' neet fra seein' Annie, an' Muther'd just dun weshin' an' was set ower fire. Sha clicks up pooaker an' cums at ma, an sha says, 'If ivver thu gans eftther that lass ageean, ah'll fell tha!' An ah nivver do'st!

How can one fail to regret the slow fading of all this in the face of advancing film-standardisation? Sad enough will it be when the younger generation are all reduced to B.B.C. English, yet even sadder is it to see them aping the gentilities of Hollywood. Reasonably enough one may like Americans; very reasonably indeed may one like East Yorkshire girls, but an Americanised East Yorkshire girl seems to me among the more awe-inspiring travesties of humanity one is likely to encounter during a long and sorely tried lifetime.

Peasant dialect and character are not the only wasting commodities in Holderness; so is the land itself, for its low, soft cliffs have been receding foot by foot, year by year, through all remembered time. Rainwater and frost, their cruellest enemies, hurl down the cliffs piecemeal in lumps of mottled umber mud to the dissolving grasp of the waves. Fishes have swum for centuries over the first church of Aldborough, while at Auburn only half a house is left of a village which at the Norman Conquest stood half a mile from the shore[8]. Stories dramatic and gruesome are handed down. When in 1786 the sea began swallowing Owthorne churchyard, skeletons and broken coffins stood out from the cliff and aged villagers tottered down to recognise by some relic the relatives and friends of former years whom they had fondly imagined safe till the Day of Judgment. The year after Waterloo the east end of the church itself crashed into the waves, revealing the tomb of some medieval magnate embalmed and buried in lead foil, strange testimony to the departed greatness of these remote manors. The church of Owthorne is now marked on ordnance maps as a point in the pale blue sea, yet if its bells, as local poets say, ring at high tide like a prelude by Debussy, I for one have never heard them.

Further south at Kilnsea a once stout parish has been gradually slimmed into a modest wedge between sea and Humber, and from this wedge the long spoon-shaped promontory of Spurn curls out southward and ends with the solitary lighthouse, which in sailing out of the Humber you encounter almost as if it stood on an islet, so long and exiguous is the strip of sand and coarse grasses – these last a vital component – connecting the Spurn with Yorkshire. The place conveys a strangely mingled sense of beauty and insecurity. To these dunes, themselves unique along the Yorkshire coast, resort the Lesser Tern, the Ring Plover and other unusual birds; here flourishes that rare and beautiful plant, the sea-holly. Yet under the long rollers ancient ports lie buried without a trace.

You stand on the strangest *ultima Thule* in England, a frail tempest-battered bank rising a foot or two above the waters, yet balanced by a feat of equilibrium between the tides from the east and the mighty flow of all Yorkshire's rivers from the west. Ever daring and dissatisfied, the headland slowly pushes southward across the estuary, leaving its neck to be broken by some abnormal tide. Assiduous and costly have been the efforts to preserve this harbourage from the north-east gales, yet in 1905-1906, and again recently, the cunning sea broke through farther north, near Easington, with ruinous effect upon wells, roads and many hundred acres of land[9].

On board ship there is seldom, in my experience, much doubt as to the moment you round the Spurn; the vessel, hitherto so calm and docile, suddenly plunges like a frightened horse; the glasses slide off the saloon tables, the stewards go in search of polite receptacles and not a few voyagers begin counting the hours to Rotterdam or Gothenburg.

Here on land, a series of hermits maintained the first beacons, one of them being found in the act of building a chapel by Henry Bolingbroke when in 1399 he landed at this place (called then Ravenspurn, but later corrupted by Shakespeare) to claim the crown.

> 'The banished Bolingbroke repeals himself
> And with uplifted arms is safe arrived
> At Ravenspurg.'

In a sober historical document the successful usurper is soon found graciously pardoning the hermit for building without license and even granting him the site. At Ravenspurn too landed Edward IV, returning in 1471 to recover his crown by force of arms from Bolingbroke's grandson. The harbour thus beloved of usurpers probably lay outside the present curve of the Spurn, which, besides growing to the south, has also shifted steadily westward during the intervening centuries.

This brief and romantic story of the emergence, prosperity and vanishing of the other lost ports, Old Ravenser and Ravenser Odd, has produced a crop of historical and geographical theories so involved and conflicting as to defy brief analysis. Weighty opinion now inclines to the view that they lie engulfed, not inside the estuary as was formerly supposed but beneath the sea itself, well to the north-east of the present Spurn. The latter and the more important of these two places arose about 1234 south of Old Ravenser upon what the envious men of Grimsby called 'a small island in the sea'. A wrecked ship afforded shelter to an enterprising trader, who sold provisions to passing vessels; a settlement rapidly sprang up, was granted a fair and a market, then chartered by Edward I contemporaneously with Hull. Between 1304 and 1326 Ravenser was sending members to Parliament; its merchants were paying considerable customs on wool and built a Chapel of St. Mary. Its chief merchant family was called Atte See, later absurdly baronialised to de la Mare. By 1355, however, we find the Abbot of Meaux being ordered to gather up and bury elsewhere the bodies of the dead uncovered by an inundation of the chapel yard. Within half a century the waters had completely reclaimed both Ravensers, and the Meaux chronicler had drawn the inevitable moral: 'their wrong-doing on the sea, their wicked works and piracies . . . provoked the wrath of God against them beyond measure.' The first effort of the fickle river to recompense Holderness for the erosion of the sea had ended in disaster. Not so the second.

During the seventeenth century an island of sand and soil began to emerge much further west, in the opposite bend of the long Humber bay and to the south of the township of Patrington. In 1668 Charles II – his jest at this unearned accretion to his dominions one would fain have heard – rented it for five pounds a year to Colonel Gilby, governor of Hull, whose descendants assisted the efforts of the river by artificial means. Accordingly by 1831 the new parish of Sunk Island, now in fact safely joined to the mainland, consisted of 6,000 acres of excellent soil, fifteen farms, many cottages and a new brick church. Since then the land has been greatly extended eastward and nature's chances of a successful riposte rendered negligible.[10]

This method of reclamation, known as warping, has, incidentally, redeemed some hundred square miles in the Humber area. The selected plot is first enclosed by an earth bank, or by hedges of brushwood and faggots locally called 'kiddies'. To this enclosure the waters are allowed to find access at high tide, deposit their burden of rich mud and then flow away. Yet nature's directer and lowlier agents are likewise achieving comparable results. The warp of the mudflats between Spurn and Sunk Island supports the *vaucheria* and other species of algae which form a cellular network, entangle blown seeds and so produce a peculiar vegetation, in its turn binding together the silt and helping to win land from the water. Here grow salt marsh plants, hairy and fleshy, with strange blooms on leaves and stem. Near the constantly wet mud spring glass-wort, seaside sedge, sea-plate grass and michaelmas daisy, while on higher and drier layers sea-arrow grass, sea plantain and scurvy grass contribute to these narrow marine gardens blooming so hardily between the contentious elements. Recently a large area of mudflat near Welwick has been planted with spartina grass to initiate the process of reclamation.

Above Sunk Island the coast lies bare and featureless until you reach Paull, a rather straggling place on various levels and divided into four parts:

High Paul and Low Paul, Paul and Paul Holme,
There never was a fair maid married in Paul Town.'

So ran a mysterious rhyme long current in Holderness, one which official glossators say sprang from the position of the church, aloof and inaccessible in the fields. This theory I find unconvincing; may we not believe the author to have been some rejected and jaundiced suitor, intent by a catch-phrase to cast aspersions of one sort or another upon the female population? I seem to remember being impressed mainly by a distant view of the oil tanks when I was

Paull Lighthouse.
(JDL)

last at Paull, but I now read that it once boasted a dockyard of some note and as late as 1812 launched the *Anson* of 74 guns, over 200 feet long and costing £140,000. At Paull Holme to the east, a fine old ivy-clad tower, part of a fortified mansion dating from about the reign of Henry VII, stands at the foot of Holme Hill, in itself a by no means dizzy eminence, but long ago artificially heightened, so it is said, in order to pass signals to the great Abbey of Thornton in Lincolnshire.

Among the lost ports of the Humber we might logically enough include Hedon, since it has been lost, not at sea but inland. Nearly two miles from the Humber, it began to trade along a natural haven in Norman times and soon afterwards, rather in the manner of Bristol, dug artificial havens either side of the town. By 1200 it boasted a canal-ring with quays ostensibly no less than a mile and a quarter in length and must have borne some resemblance to Bruges, Lübeck and Amsterdam, all ports similarly situated and planned. From this point, however, though its burgesses developed their constitution, left stacks of documents and struggled on with vast churches, Hedon's relative importance in the Humber trade declined before the rise of Hull and Ravenser Odd. Statistics given by its historian Boyle indicate that Hull was out-trading it by 1204-1206, but the bearing of these figures has been disputed. Certainly it was in decline a century later. By the Tudor age, says our saturnine commentator Leland, its day had altogether passed: 'The se crekes parting about the sayde Town did insulate it, and Shippis lay aboute the Town: but now men cum to it by 3 Bridges, where it is evident to se that sum places wher the Shippes lay be over grown with Flagges and Reades, and the Haven is very sorely decayid.'

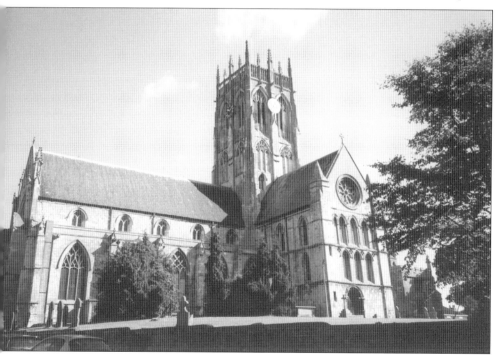

St. Augustine's church, Hedon: the King of Holderness.
(JDL)

Of its three original churches, St. Augustine's alone remains; it is one of our statelier English parish churches, well deserving for regal masculinity its popular title King of Holderness, even if its matchless consort at Patrington, the Queen, obviously got the lion's share of married life. Though the austerity of the Early English chancel has been a little vulgarised by the insertion of a sprawling Perpendicular window, these later builders also crowned the church with a huge and stately central tower, which lends the whole building something of the air of a minor cathedral.

On the south side of the town one may trace the broad, dry hollow of the Haven[11], where cows and buttercups replace the squat hulls and crowding masts of those early ships depicted on the seals of Hedon and many another venerable port. Two miles away, glimpsed through the trees, a smoke-plumed coaster sails in another century. Back in the old Town Hall the celebrated Hedon mace may be inspected; a chastely designed bauble of the reign of Henry V, it is probably the oldest and certainly the least vulgar in the country.[12] And down a little side street off Magdalen Gate a garden contains a remarkable stone cross brought many years ago from Spurn and said to have been erected there to mark the landing of Bolingbroke. But with these few meagre exceptions, only St. Augustine's truly reflects the pathos of decay; the rest of this ramshackle little town, with its dingy brick houses and pleasant old gardens, lost its greatness too many centuries ago to continue feeling sorry for itself.[13] About the Hull side of the town, vague aspirations toward futurity linger, since there an airport for the Continental lines functioned not unsuccessfully during the thirties.

That strange minor-key attraction of southern Holderness lies in large measure around the coast, which we have hitherto followed, yet between ocean and estuary are scattered many villages, some loveable and homely, some of surpassing historical and architectural interest. Enviously may we imagine the epicurean, the learned, the infallible representative of the late Herr Baedeker carefully checking the impressive wine list of the Hull Station Hotel, then leaping into his Mercedes to perambulate Holderness, grudgingly awarding one star apiece to Halsham, Winestead, Swine and Welwick, two stars to Burton Constable and a whole galaxy, comets, nebulae and all, to Patrington. Meanwhile we can but follow dimly in the wake of this demi-god with our water-bottle, our bicycle and our few modest comments.

Halsham was the original home of the Holderness Constables and its church their burial place, until, a century and a half ago, they built the domed mausoleum and, with that passion for neatness characteristic of the age, collected up the family bones and placed them in this elegant repository. In the church itself stands yet the beautiful alabaster tomb of Sir John Constable (c. 1407) with its delicate canopies surrounding the figures of angels. This may be instructively contrasted with the Winestead tomb of the Elizabethan Sir Christopher Hildyard, highly secular in *décor* and worldly wise in its motto, *Felix quem faciunt aliena pericula cautum*.[14] Poulson, the old historian of Holderness, depicted these two altar tombs upon one plate, which – had the squirearchy then been amenable to irreverent historical criticism – he might well have entitled 'Two Centuries of Progress'.

At Winestead there stood originally three interesting houses. The Hildyards' Red Hall, a typical product of the reign of Anne, contained some outstandingly fine plaster mouldings by local craftsmen. In 1936 it was demolished by the new owners, the Corporation of Hull, and the features originally salvaged were in due course destroyed in an air raid on the city.[15] The White Hall, a good, though relatively featureless, late Georgian structure, was built by the Maisters, a prosperous family of Hull merchants; they had earlier built one of the best Georgian houses now surviving in the High Street there. The third old house is the rectory, which dates from the Restoration period, some forty years after the greatest of all East Yorkshiremen had been born in its predecessor.

In 1614 the Hildyards presented to this living Andrew Marvell Senior, who gained preferment to Hull some ten years later, his famous son then being only three years of age. The giant beech tree in the garden may well date back to that century; the spring flowers and the autumnal meadow-saffron perhaps bloomed then much as now; the place seems to breathe something of that quiet, profound and subtle spirit which thence took its origins. And if in view of the obstinate dates we cannot in fact claim that this garden moulded the poet's exquisite musing on gardens, we must be content to see him revisiting his birthplace some summer night in later years, perhaps bewailing 'by the tide of Humber' the coyness of his mistress, perhaps addressing the ancestors of our glow-worms:

Ye living lamps, by whose dear light
The nightingale does sit so late,
And studying all the summer night,
Her matchless songs does meditate;

Ye country comets, that portend
No war nor prince's funeral,
Shining unto no higher end
Than to presage the grass's fall . . .

When the reading public begins to read our earlier poets for enjoyment, when even the obtuser critics no longer merely award Marvell a side-chapel in the Miltonic temple, when all recognise him as, at his best, the greatest lyrist of our greatest age of lyric poetry, then I fear, Winestead and Nun Appleton may become literary shrines like Dove Cottage or Haworth; the charabanc parties will surge, the ice-cream drip, the accordions wail . . . yet if such bardic recognition comes, it should scarcely precede the second millennium A.D. *Après nous, le déluge.*

Amid places of slightly lesser interest, the admirable fragment of the one-time nunnery church at Swine contains, in the Hilton family chapel, the finest series of medieval alabaster tombs in the Riding. Separating this chapel from the north aisle stands the remarkable carved screen, Flemish rather than Italianate, erected by Lord Darcy shortly before the Pilgrimage of Grace, which event spelt such disaster to him and his family. At Welwick – or rather at Ploughland, now a farm on the Patrington road – lived the Wright family, two of whose members, John and Christopher, attained great notoriety as foundation-members of the Gunpowder Plot and perished in the final desperate rising which followed its collapse. In the church of Welwick you will find the brass figures of their half-brother, William, and his wife, Anne, according to this inscription a very different couple, 'who after they had lived lovingly together ye space of 50 yeares in the feare of God and love of Men, finished a faire pilgrimage to a Joyfull Paradice . . . *Memoria Justi vivet in aeternum'*. Needless to remark, the brass engraver has succeeded in giving them expressions of intolerable piety, in striking contrast with that famous illustrated tract of 1605, which represents their plotter brothers as a pair of jovial but cunning fanatics with peaked beards and mustachios, high-crowned hats and stage-jesuit expressions. Also at Welwick is a quite magnificent, though badly mutilated, tomb-canopy, obviously once the memorial of a man of note and brought hither from elsewhere – tradition says from Burstall Priory.

Of Patrington one is prompted either to write ten pages of superlatives or else simply to declare it the loveliest parish church one has ever seen, a claim most unlikely to be dismissed as mere local enthusiasm by any traveller who takes the trouble to reach this remote corner of Holderness. Patrington is all grace and light and slender femininity, the quintessence, the *flos florum* of English Decorated architecture. Its size, elegance and elaboration correspond with no merely material factors, though it was indeed built as a unity about 1310-1349, on a rich manor belonging to the See of York. Again, at a rather later date, one

Robert of Patrington appears, perhaps significantly, as master mason, or, as we should say, architect, of York Minster. It clearly seems the concept of a single mind, since, however fascinating in variety of detail, however transcending the mechanised repetitions of a modern millionaire-donor's product, the whole structure shows such clean harmony, unity, balance, proportion as to compel the admission: 'Here for once Gothic architecture becomes Classical.' If Hull and Hedon have the massivity of minor cathedrals, Patrington is the perfect *miniature* cathedral, with many a feature – double-aisled transepts, a rose window, a transept-chapel, a magnificent range of both interior and exterior carving – quite uncommon or almost unique amongst mere parish churches.

The unity of this complex structure is in large part achieved by the wide graceful swing of Decorated arches set upon slender eight-clustered columns with exquisite, naturally foliated capitals; they spell a unity almost un-marred save by the fifteenth-century builders who intruded their great Perpendicular east window. Of the many detailed curiosities, the famous Easter Sepulchre with the three sleeping soldiers, the angels and the Risen Lord, is a wonderfully preserved specimen of the crude contemporary English figure-sculpture, an art unworthy of the great architecture which it served. The exterior of this church forms no mere reverse of the fabric; its proportions are admirable, its

St. Patrick's church, Patrington:
the Queen of Holderness.
(JDL)

gargoyles and anecdotal figures profuse but disciplined, its high tower crowned by a spire of consummate grace. This last feature owes its effect to the delicate octagon with which the architect has surrounded the base of the spire, a device thought meretricious by Freeman and the moralist critics, but surely justified here by excellent spacing and complete harmony with the character of the whole.

Patrington would alone repay the visit of any cultivated man to the East Riding, but it is hardly fair game for novices in architectural appreciation; it will spoil them for the average product, make them ask why these brilliantly experimental yet spasmodically inconstant communities and masons could not more often visualise their dreams as single-souled unities and then achieve them, by a mighty effort of will and application, inside a single working life. The historical answer to this query would, of course, involve no great profundities concerning the medieval mind and technique: it seems well nigh as hopeless to demand this from our ancestors as to demand great art from the victims of the modern production-belt. Yet here and there the feat was almost achieved, and nowhere more nearly than at Patrington.

Burton Constable, as befits the seigneurial mansion of Holderness, may claim unquestioned primacy among the great houses of the East Riding. The various branches of the Constable family at Halsham, Everingham, Flamborough and elsewhere have been among the great landowners of the district since the eleventh century. Tradition connects one corner of the present mansion with the reign of Stephen and recent investigation has in fact proved it to contain a rubble wall some eight feet in thickness. Both the great central block and the two wings nevertheless dated originally from the reign of Henry VIII. Georgian rebuilding did little to alter the exteriors, but the majority of the rooms were remodelled about 1770 by William Constable, a cultivated and travelled maecenas who acquired a large part of the remarkable collection of pictures. Capability Brown, whose accounts are preserved in the voluminous family archives, could make nothing very romantic out of the flat park which surrounds the mansion, yet its ancient copses and its long lakes provide a dignified setting, appropriate to the landscape of Holderness. This water lies westward of the house and, apart from its five-arched bridge, is scarcely visible from the upper windows themselves, so flat is the immediate terrain. Farther westward still, the land begins to undulate and from its highest point, Roe Hill, affords an outlook of unwonted breadth, embracing Beverley, the Wolds, Hull, the Humber and Lincolnshire. The park once contained a herd of *bos urus*, the wild ox still to be seen at Chillingham, but destroyed here by a distemper in the mid-eighteenth century. Here we should probably have come a century ago when, apart from five hundred fallow deer, the Constables maintained eighty or ninety red deer and trained them for hunting on special diets of old oats and hay, linseed, isinglass and ivy-leaves. Once run down, the animal was seized by the huntsman before sustaining permanent damage, placed alone with a few holly branches to gnaw, until, after two or three days, he recovered from his fatigue sufficiently to partake of further sport. 'To hunt three days a week,' says our reverent Poulson, 'requires eleven brace. The splendid runs which so frequently occur are generally faithfully related in all the provincial papers.'

The hall is best approached from the Sproatley-Marton road, which affords the casual passer-by a satisfactory view of the east facade, with its two wings. It is at present impracticable to open the house to the public except on special occasions, yet no tolerable account of the East Riding could omit some brief mention of its more outstanding treasures[16]. These have in no sense been diminished since Poulson described them in 1840, but considerable rearrangements and acquisitions, quite apart from his own doubtful attributions, render his account of little present service. In turn, the present writer, though kindly entertained and helped by the owner, cannot claim to have spent those many days in the house which an exhaustive and confident description would demand.

The excellent condition of the fabric and its collections would strike any observer aware of the harsh vicissitudes and problems of recent years. During the last war, this area became a favourite unloading point for irresolute enemy airmen attacking Hull; literally hundreds of bombs fell in the near vicinity. The damage, together with that arising from a military canteen in the Entrance Hall, proved expensive but superficial. Peacetime responsibilities remain gigantic. As an irreducible minimum, eleven-and-a-half acres of lawn have to be cut, while a heavy fall of snow on the two-and-a-half acres of roof demands the immediate services of numerous workmen. At least twenty rooms, mostly of great size, contain *objets d'art* of the first rank and must be heated at frequent intervals, while only a captious critic would censure an admitted failure to wind every one of the 174 clocks at present in the house.

The Chinese Room has few surviving counterparts, though the character of its *décor* will provide few surprises for those familiar with the depleted yet still attractive Pavilion at Brighton. The lively dragons which cling to the window frames are matched by a number of similar motives, especially by those of the great gilt Chippendale chair, surely the most fantastic of the master's essays in *chinoiserie*. The painted wallpaper and the lacquer cabinets are both of striking beauty and aptitude. The Red Drawing Room has a large assembly of family portraits, very mixed in their artistic merits, but including some good eighteenth-century pastels. The four sets of miniatures include one item attributed to Holbein himself and another which appears on amateur inspection to be a Nicholas Hilliard. The Blue Drawing Room is mainly remarkable for a number of Dutch cabinet pictures, some of gallery rank, by Wouwerman, Cuyp, Both, van der Vinne and other familiar masters.

A solitary Jordaens supplies the contrasting note.

The main collection of paintings hangs in the Staircase Hall, a room of immense proportions, surrounded on three sides by a staircase and gallery which cling to the outer wall with no other visible means of support. A nervous earlier owner who inserted a bracket at one point merely provided a little moral reassurance, since the bracket fails by half an inch to support any of the weight. The soaring walls with their serried rows of canvases remind one of those princely art galleries which the younger Teniers was so fond of depicting. The most attractive item is a *Boar Hunt* attributed to Rubens, a canvas of moderate size, recently cleaned and now revealed in all its brilliant vitality. The other piece assigned to the Flemish master is a study of a lioness and her cubs; it does not possess, at least in its present uncleaned state, the same appeal. Beneath the staircase is a large portrait group by Edward Bird, showing Louis XVIII soon after his restoration to the throne, attended by numerous celebrities. Prominent among these stands his friend Sir Thomas Hugh Clifford Constable, who kept the exiled King here at Burton Constable for nearly two years of his long banishment. From the gallery one may enter the suite of rooms occupied by this stout and stodgy royalty: the State Boudoir, Bedroom and Dressing Room, still furnished in a full-blown French style of the period. In the State Bedroom are some striking portraits of Charles I, Henrietta Maria and their children by Henry Stone, a very successful imitator of Vandyke. Far more to a quiet English taste is the Dining Room below, with its olive green walls, exquisite mouldings and white statuary. Under this last heading we may include the plaster bas-reliefs by William Collins, the anatomy of his Bacchanal figures displaying extraordinary subtlety and correctness. In Yorkshire there are scores of superb Georgian rooms, but it would be hard to find more than one or two which might seriously be compared with this. The great Entrance Hall contains a carving of foliage by Grinling Gibbons, so delicate that it shakes in the wind when the main doors are opened; the Ballroom has an Adam ceiling and a marble mantelpiece in replica of one in the Doge's Palace. In the South Wing are some charming small rooms, one completely panelled in Tudor oak and giving some notion of the interior before its remodelling by William Constable. The bedrooms are furnished in a manner worthy of the state apartments; they contain pictures – especially the Lancrets and the Vernet – which many of us small amateurs would be glad to have in places of honour.

Perhaps the most remarkable parts of the collection are to be seen in the Long Gallery, itself a type of room common enough on the upper floors of Tudor mansions, but now seldom seen so perfectly preserved and appointed as at Burton Constable. Its enormous plaster ceiling is the original, with scores of pendants moulded in as many non-repetitive designs. The mantelpiece is a *tour de force* of marble inlay by the brothers Bartoli, who spent some time at work in the house. The painted glass in the gable-window belongs to the fourteenth or early fifteenth century; it has a Continental flavour and is perhaps more likely to derive from the family's French connections than from some local monastery. In this room are three portraits attributed with varying degrees of confidence to Holbein. The finest depicts Thomas Cromwell, his hard face a fitting subject for this restrained but remorseless objectivity; the others are portraits of Sir Thomas More (an interesting and little-known sidelight on the great man) and of Henry VIII's learned secretary, Sir Brian Tuke. The Erasmus, though almost as impressive, is claimed only as 'School of Holbein'. Also in this alcove hangs a contemporary picture of that famous humanist and Bishop of Durham, Cuthbert Tunstall, whose family was allied to the Constables of his day. Another fine Tudor portrait is the full-length of the celebrated Jane Dormer, Duchess of Feria, a companion of Queen Mary Tudor, who married a follower of King Philip, went into exile when Elizabeth came to the throne, helped English papalist *émigrés* on the Continent and,

during her long widowhood, founded a Spanish monastery. The portrait of Mary Queen of Scots at the opposite end of the room was given by her to one of her several English gaolers. The chief creator of the collections, William Constable, is commemorated nearby in a pastel-portrait of outstanding merit; characteristically, he appears in the familiar costume of Jean Jacques Rousseau. This room also houses a large assembly of gilded Restoration furniture which would look unduly ostentatious in any less magnificent room.

The aesthetic affluence of these eighteenth- and early nineteenth-century Constables may somewhat paradoxically be connected with the steady Catholic tradition which had caused their forbears so much suffering in penal times. Instead of buying expensive seats in Georgian Parliaments and wallowing in the public life from which their religion debarred them, they were happily able to concentrate on landlordism and art collecting. Thus the resplendent little chapel, where a service is still held weekly by the family chaplain, may be claimed in more than one sense as the centre of the household and of the family tradition[17]. That the course of religion did not always run smoothly may be deducted from the priest's hole, an unusually elaborate and spacious one with a long passage running beneath an upstairs gallery and entered by a loose board in the flooring. The intervals since the Reformation when no mass has been said in or around the Hall have been short indeed.

These last few inadequate pages are frankly intended to convince the reader that Burton Constable would honour any district of England, even the Dukeries themselves, and that it forms as primary a monument of civilisation as a medieval castle or minster. Between the end of cathedral building and the triumph of the railway engine, there came three wonderful centuries during which European culture, having groped and tottered awhile, soared to new peaks of achievement. It is that age which struck a delicate balance between the hieratic symbolism of the past and our own sensate, materialistic, anaesthetic cult of mass comfort. In England it was the age of the great house, when the aristocracy, armed somewhat slenderly with a good rent-roll, a moderate classical education and an inadequate tour of Italy, nevertheless drew into its orbit many of the finest artists and works of art which Europe has ever produced. Today this aristocracy is being liquidated simultaneously with the spending-margins of its more obvious cultural legatees, the professional classes. The double revolution leaves the problem of executorship largely to state agencies, whose short-term national interests happen to lie in the seizure (by death duties) and exchange of all such mobile resources for food-purchasing dollars. And – a final ingredient for tragedy – all this destruction of aristocratic cultural monuments happens at a time when their lesson of cool taste and craftsmanship (as opposed to the pseudo-messianic chaos and charlatanry of much twentieth-century culture) would exercise a sane and steadying influence upon creators and contemplators alike.

The fact remains that this particular type of monument is easy to dissipate and hard to conserve. The great house is not the Great Pyramid; it has to be forever patched or it will fall to ruin. It is also in large part as mobile as it is fragile. It can be exported quietly and piecemeal, even though – to any man with an inkling of civilised value – such action has little more to commend itself than the export of cathedrals. Hitherto, despite the immense and spontaneous interest shown of late by all classes of society in accessible country houses, the reaction of public authority has been ineffectual, indeed derisory. The fine phrases of royal commissions remain on paper. The National Trust can accept no house unless the quixotic owner will also provide an enormous endowment; the galleries and museums can at best only acquire a few fragments from what is essentially an organic unity; the democratic politician finds it unrewarding to expend much energy in the cause of preservation. Whatever the ultimate outcome, the state of such a house as Burton Constable around the year 1985 will provide a searching index to the cultural flexibility of British social democracy. Will it still provide witness to the traditions of honour and public service, to the discernment and conscientious artistry of our forbears – the best things they reach out to us across the centuries? Or will it by then have gone to buy the nation a few days' breakfast cereals, complete with Walt Disney designs on every cardboard packet? Was ever the sale of a birthright for a mess of pottage more brutally and literally threatened?[18]

FOOTNOTES

1 The Bayle Gate, now incorporating a museum, is open to the public.
2 The Roman mosaics are excellently displayed in the Hull and East Riding Museum, High Street, Hull.
3 Burton Agnes Hall is now open on a regular basis to the public, English Heritage is now responsible for the Old Hall. The Long Gallery was skilfully restored by Francis Johnson in two phases, 1951 (before the publication of Dickens's book) and 1974.
4 The house was left to Simon Cunliffe-Lister by Marcus Wickham-Boynton and is extremely well managed by the Hon Susan Cunliffe-Lister, who has considerably improved the gardens. Marcus Wickham-Boynbon's fine collection of modern art is still displayed.
5 Driffield is now a much smarter town. For information on its interesting history and features see David Neave, *Driffield: A Town Trail* (1981).
6 Driffield has now commemorated the famous printer in the name of Fawcett Gardens.
7 Dickens is paying a compliment to his colleague, K. A. MacMahon, whose guide, *The Church of St. Mary, Kirkburn*, had been published in 1953.
8 Auburn Farm survives.
9 The future of Spurn is a subject of continuing concern, but, in spite of pessimistic forecasts and crises, it remains accessible from the mainland. Dickens is referring to the severe flooding of 1953.
10 For the story of Sunk Island see John Whitehead, *Sunk Island* (Beverley, 1991).
11 The (West) Haven was regrettably filled in and substantially levelled c.1970. Only faint indications of the central hollow

remain. See also K. J. Allison, *The East Riding of Yorkshire Landscape* (1976).

12 Hedon's remarkable civic collection of silver can be seen by groups by arrangement with the Town Clerk. See Peter A. Garvey, *The Hedon Silver* (revised Martin T. Craven and John Markham, Beverley, 2000).

13 Since Dickens wrote, there has been a much increased awareness of Hedon's history and architecture. The once drab Souttergate has been restored to its original attractive appearance as a street of good Georgian houses. The green belt between Hedon and Hull has considerably decreased. Salt End has developed as a massive complex.

14 Happy is the man who is made cautious by the attempts (or perils) of others.

15 Paradoxically the demolition of the Red Hall (apart from the stable block) led to the foundation (by Colonel R. A. Alec-Smith) of the Georgian Society for East Yorkshire, an organisation which has stimulated interest in the area's architectural riches. Colonel Alec-Smith took up post-war residence in the former Rectory, Winestead, where he installed a number of items from bombed or demolished Georgian houses in Hull's High Street and also doors from the Red Hall. Dickens is surprisingly dismissive of the attractive White Hall. It is now considered to have been the inspiration of Winifred Holtby's fictional Maythorpe Hall in her famous novel, *South Riding*.

16 Burton Constable Hall, under the control of the Burton Constable Foundation since 1992, is open regularly to the public. Many changes have been made to the interior seen by Dickens, an energetic and intelligent conservation policy pursued, and former artefacts from the house re-acquired. A new guide has been re-issued in 2002. A separate list of paintings is also available.

17 The chapel is no longer in regular use. An earlier chapel, in use during penal times, was in the south tower.

18 A danger which Dickens could not have foreseen was the plan to build a massive council estate near Burton Constable Hall to accommodate Hull residents needing rehousing, particularly as a consequence of the demolition of sub-standard property. The idea so enraged Brigadier Raleigh Chichester-Constable that he threatened to burn the house down. In the event the plan was abandoned and the Bransholme estate developed in its place. Now under excellent management, Burton Constable Hall is in far better condition than it has been for years.

Beverley

Beverley, with some account of which I propose to conclude this essay, is the administrative capital of the East Riding, yet belongs strictly speaking neither to Holderness nor to the Wolds. It lies centrally upon the narrow strip of ground between the Hull and the first waves of the hills. You should certainly approach it from the latter direction, perhaps by my regular Whitsun walk from Bishop Burton (that most utterly paintable village of East Yorkshire) across to the Westwood, an ancient common pasturage and the scene of many a sanguinary annual football match between the men of Beverley and those of the neighbouring townships. Having traversed the meadows with their trails of blackthorn and bevies of lambs, you first reach this great rolling expanse near Burton Bushes, a strip of genuine primeval forest, the *silva Deiorum* of Bede, and then glimpse from afar off the grey shapes of Beverley's majestic churches high above the dark medley of common roofs. Passing the black windmill which lies disused like an old ship amid the green ocean, you come upon the Tan Gallop, a track made of parings from the old tanneries of Beverley and used to train racehorses from the important stables situated here. Leaving the race-course itself on your left, you pass the spot where the Pilgrims of Grace held their first riotous assemblies, and enter the town by a little street till recently called Ducking Stool Lane and leading to North Bar Without.

This town was never walled, yet boasted 'many fair Gates of Brike', of which North Bar alone survives – a domesticated little structure, by no means redolent of martial clangour.[1] Having attained North Bar Within and passed a gracious row of Georgian houses, you immediately reach St. Mary's, a church which an unfortunate essayist who has already exhausted his superlatives on Patrington, yet needs more for the Minster, can by no means adequately praise. In sober truth, few of our smaller English counties can rank even a single building alongside these three masterpieces.

The extreme massivity of the central tower and its piers represents the townsmen's reply to the collapse of the tower during a service one tragic April day in 1520. The next crisis, a period of Victorian restoration by the Pugins, passed off with surprisingly innocuous, even beneficial results, so that we can still enjoy St. Mary's uninhibited by visions of sidewhiskers, enjoy the richly sculptured doorway and polygonal turrets[2] of the west end, the ogival south porch, the intricately woven bays of the north choir aisle, the superb late Perpendicular font presented by a local draper and his wife in 1530, the delightfully carved screens and misericordes in the choir. The communal character of the rebuilding is finely illustrated by the inscriptions on the various pillars of the northern nave arcade: 'Xlay and hys wyffe made these 2 pyllors and a halffe'; 'Thes to pyllors made gud wyffys God reward thaym'; 'Thys pillor made the meynstryls'. This last one, the celebrated Minstrels' Pillar, has five curious little musicians' figures in their original colouring and placed high up on corbels just beneath the capital.

I suggested that the puginisation of this church might be held beneficial; this depends upon whether or not you admire the big, romantic flying buttresses which these Victorians, more medieval than the Middle Ages, attached to the south transept to prevent subsidence, or so they said. Before arriving at a decision, compare the present exterior with the pre-Pugin plate in Poulson's *Beverlac* and then frankly admit, as I do, that the Pugins caught you napping, that had you not been informed, you would never have guessed this significant addition to be modern.

Just beyond St. Mary's you reach the Saturday Market and need not regret it overmuch if the busy turmoil happens not to rage today, for Beverley is a land wherein every afternoon is Saturday, a far better state of affairs than the permanent Sunday afternoon which reigns over certain of the more dowageresque suburbs of Oxford and Cambridge. Beverley town is a secular-minded little gossiping busybody, not a bit appalled by the presence of its two glorious churches and not very seriously pretending to be a provincial capital. You sense its spirit fairly accurately in one of those several public houses where farmers, agents for agricultural machinery and commercial travellers transact business over their pints, or where, in the tipsters' classic phrase, 'jockeys and trainers assemble daily'. In these latter and more equine circles you will still discover, quite apart from the mere touts and theorists, much of that genuine knowledge of horseflesh for which Yorkshire has so long earned international fame.[3] In short, townee Beverley, as distinct from ecclesiastical Beverley, may savour a little of fish-and-chips, sporting pinks and chain-stores, but we would not seek to refine her any more than to refine a cockney comedienne, for that would be to miss the point. And Beverley has never been without its dignified provincial society – in the last generation, for example, those fine period-figures, Canon Nolloth and Admiral Walker, the latter of whom lived in the old house overlooking the Westwood and many years ago employed a late academic associate of mine to educate his sons, I believe on a carefully prescribed but indigestible diet of Aristotle. Beverley has, too, certain local artists and craftsmen of repute, some of whom still maintain notable family traditions.

The Saturday Market sports a market-cross resembling a bandstand and presented by two local M.P.s in an age when such functionaries were expected to do more for their constituents than deliver intermittent and amateur lectures on economics. Again, hereabouts, there once ministered to our barbaric youth an Ancient Gaumont British temple, wherein the solitary old Druid seemed personally to perform every rite attendant upon the worship of the Divine Chaplin – even to the sale of cigarettes, which we young devotees smoked under the blissful cloak of darkness . . .

From the Saturday Market to the Wednesday

Market and thence to the south end of the town and the Minster is no long walk, and for us this must be the end of the journey, since whatever else needs most to be said of Beverley and the East Riding may conveniently be said in what is by far the greatest work of man in our province. Though not officially a cathedral, Beverley would be ranked by any competent authority among the great cathedrals of western Europe and I have known two able students of church architecture, neither local men nor wine-bibbers, having just toured all France, and with the splendours of Chartres, Beauvais, Amiens fully in mind, declare in cool daylight that their journeys had led them to nothing lovelier than Beverley. No man may reasonably weigh one beauty against another, yet I must confess to finding the comparison with Chartres productive of some interesting, if rather cloudy, reflections. Chartres is the Catholic Church, organised on every side by logic and law, yet within this compass luxuriously human, infinitely anthropomorphic. It seethes with the figures of men and women; it hurls them up in fountains, while yet holding them within its great architectonic scheme. It is not merely the Bible in stone; it is a petrification of all Christian and pagan history. Early English Beverley seems by contrast a proto-Protestant; it suggests the crags at the mountain top or, more properly, the bare glade in early spring, where the individual soul stands in loneliness face-to-face with its own sense of God. I call it half Protestant, the symbol of *ecclesia anglicana*, remembering how pleasantly it harmonised with both our Carolines and our Victorians, yet might one not rather regard the spirit which informed its builders as a survival of the Celtic strain in English Christianity? Despite the Roman philosophies and forms of administration, did not this more truly native strain continue to grow underground and then, in the thirteenth century, when English literature also broke its long silence, did it not escape from the closer forms of Continental tutelage to create these grave, sweet harmonies? The

north and south portals of Chartres – how significantly one thinks so much of portals there, so little at Beverley – are the logical outcome of the somewhat earlier classical schools at Chartres. They are up-to-date and boldly forward-looking; they stand on the threshold of Christian Humanism; they have been understandably compared with a *summa theologica*, but they resemble more closely the luxuriant *Encyclopedia* by Vincent of Beauvais. Beverley, sparsely clothed in the tightly-curled foliage of March, has all the backward-looking qualities of this early spring, full of the memory of distant summers and autumns; it turns to look back at the fabled austerities of St. Cuthbert, the half-forgotten dream of Lindisfarne and Jarrow, the distant age when the periphery of Europe achieved Christianity with the freshness and heroism of the recently-retired warrior-band, yet lacked the technique to express itself in cathedrals.

Thus warmed to the theme, one might well proceed to elaborate similarly resonant comparisons between Beverley and other members of the English Gothic family. It has something in common with the musical grace of Lincoln and with the crowned pomp of York, more still, when you set aside superficial traits, with Salisbury (still quiring to the young-eyed cherubims!), yet in the last resort it stands without close peers. We who have had the fortune to form our first architectural notions around its walls should perhaps be the last to work out parallels, the first to rest content, praising God and man for the very uniqueness of our heritage.

Here in Beverley itself, if you think St. Mary's a beautiful *bourgeoise*, you will admit the Minster to be a *grande dame*, one whose high lineage dates back to Bede's master, St. John of Beverley, or, more tangibly, to the foundation grant by which King Athelstan fulfilled his vow, after the saint had kept his part of the bargain and enlisted a sufficient measure of celestial aid to give Athelstan the victory at Brunanburgh. From this time, too, Beverley became the sanctuary of the North, a rather unenviable distinction in view of the fact that, during the sixty years before Henry had the courage to abolish this sacred thuggery, no less than 186 murderers and homicides, together with 54 felons and countless lesser offenders, successfully claimed the peace of St. John. Near the altar you will note the thousand-year-old Frid Stool, the centre point of the sanctuary, having gained which a criminal could only be molested under the very direst penalties. Radiating outwards from the Minster were six concentric circles of protection with gradually decreasing penalties for infringement, the outermost of them a mile away, the next marked by stone crosses, some of which can still be traced by the roadside if you know where to look.

Meanwhile St. John became a premier saint of the North, one whose lands the Conqueror himself dare not harry, one of the three under whose banners, flown from a high mast on a cart, the Yorkshireman trounced the Scots at the Battle of the Standard in 1138. About this time Archbishop Thurstan chartered the town; it soon became a port by cutting the canal, Beverley Beck, which connects it with the River Hull a mile away, and where the barges still load and unload at the staithes with little more than medieval rapidity.[4]

Little remains of the earlier churches of St. John, the present one springing substantially from three later periods: the chancel and all four transepts rank with Salisbury as the classic exemplar of Early English; the famous west front and towers are Perpendicular; the nave, a somewhat more complex structure between these two extremes, has eight of its eleven bays in an Early Decorated style closely assimilated to the Early English, but with a variety of aisle windows, those on the south side admirably exemplifying the local Flamboyant manner to which reference has previously been made. This nave, though admittedly the least exciting of the three portions, has suffered undue criticism at the hands of the formidable Freeman[5] on account of the somewhat

depressed character of its vaulting. Yet is it not this demand for pointedness in all things just part of the Early English complex which afflicted our predecessors to the exclusion of admiration for other styles? Is not a nave the half-conscious effort of a people sprung from the forest to express its mystery and rhythmic recession, rather than a line of pointed rockets directed at heaven? Is our enjoyment of Gothic not better accompanied by the thought of Sibelius walking in the forest, rather than by the image of the Rev. Dr. Fuzzbuzz (d.1880) aspiring to get to heaven on the uncomfortable point of a very pointed arch?

As for this gradual tree-like curve at Beverley, I find it well suited to Decorated composition, enhancing rather than otherwise the loftiness of arcade and triforium.

The chancel contains features of most diverse interest: incomparable Early English double staircase in the north aisle, the clever and unique construction of the lesser transept-crossing, with its series of projecting stages, the Rabelaisian series of misericords – pigs playing bagpipes, monkeys doctoring bed-ridden goats, bear-baiting, hunting, tippling, morris dancing, all that gross imagination and coarse secularity of the average medieval mind, which peeps at us furtively around the most sacred corners and which yearly at the Feast of Fools invaded the church itself.

Immediately to the north of the altar towers the famous Percy tomb, which one might venture to call the most significant *objet d'art* of late medieval England. From the heraldry and figures of this great ogival canopy the commentators deduce much of secondary importance. They seem to prove that this is the tomb of Eleanor Fitzalan, daughter of the first Lord Percy; that, though she died in 1328, it was probably not erected until some eleven years later. Of the decoration, while admitting the exquisite character of its detail, they commonly use the terms 'decadent' and 'overburdened', again betraying that

Early English complex, so insensitive to the enormous and tragic aspirations of this wonderful fourteenth century, which, as readers will long ago have sensed, was the golden age of our East Riding. With the Percy tomb we are indeed far beyond that Early English springtime which soars in stone glades around it; we are in the riotous midsummer week when the unheard-of threatens, when even more daring fantastic growths seem about to rise from the startled earth. This monument – and by more certain routes than a mere Flamboyant or the fussy detail of the German woodcarvers – seeks to overleap the trammels of the medieval line, to conceive decoration not merely in terms of timid little rows of dogtooth or ball-flower, but decoration on a daring and truly significant scale, in other words to reach by a single glorious bound of the imagination the splendour of the Baroque, nearly three centuries before its appointed hour. So this obscure artist bade fair to equal the feat of his younger contemporary Chaucer, who also leapt out of his age and achieved direct contact with Elizabethan and Stuart minds. In the face of such an achievement, the Early English shows but the young seed time, and the Perpendicular, which finally won the day, a more timid, an autumn frost before mid-summer's glory had broken, a blank refusal to fulfil a vast promise, the *gran rifiuto* of English plastic art. Explain the refusal how you will – by the Black Death, the dominance of the glass-painter, the coming of the *parvenu* wool-merchant patron, the new bare-souled mysticism of the *devotio moderna*, the pre-Reformation pietism – it seems to believe in the face of this astonishing canopy that here the creative mind was on the point of achieving fresh concepts when somehow the spiritual drive failed.

Occasional visitors to the Minster often miss its greatest experience, which is only to be gained by ascending to the broad top of the stone altar screen. This not very lofty point of vantage is reached by a winding staircase, steep, dark, but mercifully short, in the north choir aisle. From the point where one emerges, the Percy tomb may be more minutely inspected than from ground-level. More important, it is possible from the screen not merely to view but to *experience* the whole church, to be lifted up into the bosom of the stone forest and made to feel its child. This is a place to visit when one has read and forgotten guidebooks, shaken off human companions and reached a state of mind which can bear to make a solitary entrance into very august company.

The most complete exterior view of the church is obtained by walking a hundred yards or more southward from the south-west tower, and then looking back across the small field which may once have contained the manor-house of the medieval archbishops. The picture is hence dominated by the late West Front and its towers – a front which might indeed provoke a hostile response to my phrase 'the great refusal', because it is at once Perpendicular and aspiring, Perpendicular which is really perpendicular, and not fundamentally horizontal like the West Front of York and most other products of this misnamed style. These are the perfect west towers; they embody to the full those mysterious yet logical space-relations which set the mind at rest with a deep sense of finality and satisfaction. It is as if the draughtsman had said, 'The business of a tower is to suggest height: let us then add illusion to mere measurements.' Accordingly he built twin towers which the measuring-line declares nearly forty feet lower than their opposite numbers at York, towers which nevertheless *look* as high again. For his masterstroke he has incurred thunder-bolts of unusually heavy calibre from the Olympian moralists. Between the towers he has raised the end of the gable high above the nave roof which lies behind it, building at this dizzy level a long chamber which runs across the entire width of the towers. Now in my impression this raised gable, however little integrated with the nave, is the supreme height-making feature of the west front, which front the designer was clearly thinking out – as gothic designers so often did – as a *tour de force* in isolation. The original mind, entrusted with a specific task, has here refused to water down his grand design at the behest of his defunct predecessors: he says in effect that we cannot have it both ways.

From the summit of one of these towers the view can be breath-taking – at least if you have breath left after the toilsome ascent, one of those many such which should give the foundation of a Cathedral Lift Society a high priority within any sensible scheme of ecclesiastical reform.

As you step on to the leads, the land shines green, luxuriant and boundless on all sides; innumerable hedgerows intertwine snake-wise in diminishing perspective; the nearer woods stand apart, separated by park-like stretches and open champaign, the further merge into undifferentiated forest land, its glades subdued to a velvet softness by the interposed veil of vapour. Around the western and northern horizon the Wolds throw their great arms, while, to the east, coastal hazes hide, yet suggest and foreshadow the sea, as would a ghost lingering above its tomb. Southward, above the long Humber, where the clustering chimneys billow their fumes, the sunlight strives to gild this commercial dust into a halo of beauty. Through the late afternoon farmer, husbandman, docker, fisherman and factory worker are going home all over the thousand square miles of our Riding; there begins that short interval of peace between the life of the day and that of the night.

Now pulled small and compact, its red and grey roofs gathered into a mere garden plot around these towers, Beverley lies quiet and neat as a hamlet, its traffic-rumour and gossiping tongues have faded to less than a whisper, its places, gardens and pinnacles assumed their true Lilliputian proportions. Here and there amid the patch-work of tiles a smoke plume rapidly disperses before the lightest west wind. Gulls scatter across the foreground on their storm-boding journey to inland meadows, while still the bored pigeons launch themselves periodically from their favourite gargoyles and then with a few easy turns of the wing recover some high sheltered niche in the sun.

Closer, far closer to life and reality than these ephemeral shadows, there stretches beneath us that leaden-backed, stone-ribbed Being of the Ages upon whose towering horns we precariously stand. This is the colossus, the sphinx, the alpha and the omega of our land. It ushered in that age, the so-called Later Middle Age, when the East Riding made its sole great contribution to the sum of man's spiritual wealth, the one age when lord and canon, burgher and peasant could clothe their aspirations in material beauty, in the art-forms linking us provincial men with the European civilisation which gave our humanity birth, the art which forges the sacramental bond between us poor earth-bound animals and our superhuman destiny. The most vital parts of ourselves our unaided wills can hardly fashion; the wind of the spirit bloweth where it listeth, and who can say when, in thronged and threadbare city, on lost wold farm and vale fenland, along wasting sea cliff and marsh-bordered estuary, a new understanding will quicken our drowsy hearts into fresh creativity and love?

FOOTNOTES
1   Beverley originally had four gates or 'bars'.
2   The turrets are Victorian; the originals are in Champney Road, Beverley, and in King Street, Woodmansey.
3   Beverley no longer has any racing stables.
4   The Beck has since ceased to be used commercially but there are current plans for its restoration as an attractive and historic feature.
5   Edward Augustus Freewan, who wrote an introduction to Robert Farren's *Cathedral Cities: York, Lincoln and Beverley* (1896).

Brantingham.
(JDL)

Holme-on-Spalding-Moor.
(JDL)

Pocklington.
(JDL)

Brandesburton.
(JDL)

Index of places in or near the East Riding

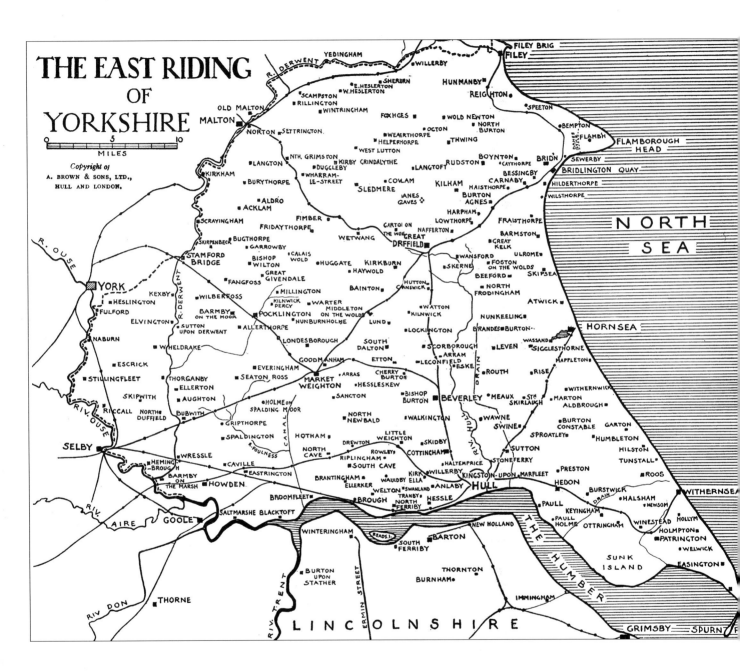

THE EAST RIDING OF YORKSHIRE

0 5 10
MILES

Copyright of
A. BROWN & SONS, LTD.,
HULL AND LONDON.